# gracious living™

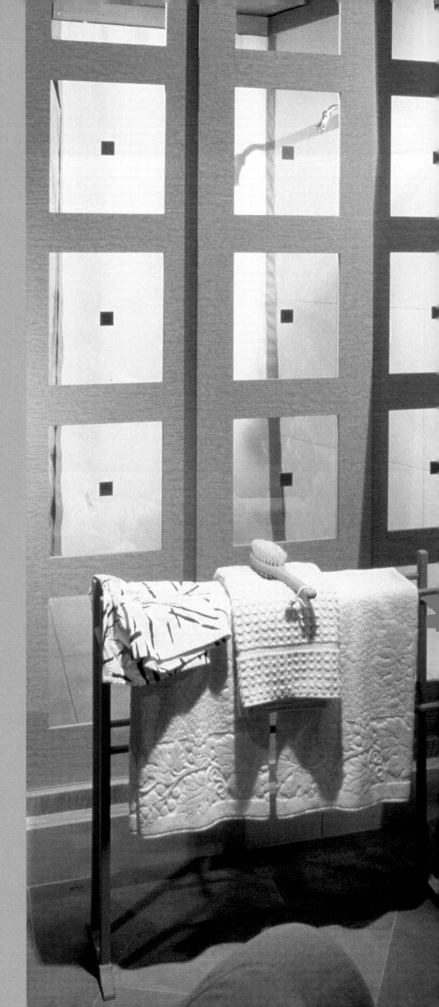

THIS BOOK, FILLED WITH INSPIRATION, IDEAS, fantasy, and reality, brings a host of wonderful products together for the first time. We at Kohler Co., with our 124-year history in the plumbing industry, are pleased to present this select group of manufacturers who make up our Kohler Coordinates program.

Consistency of design, quality, and function are the criteria that distinguish each Kohler Coordinates partner. Along with Kohler Co.'s own kitchen and bath family of businesses—including Ann Sacks Tile and Stone, Canac Kitchens, and Robern Cabinetry—we're please to have Sub-Zero, Dutch Boy Paint, Dacor, Daltile, and Wilsonart International.

Whether you're fine-tuning your kitchen, creating an intimate master bath, or designing a fun-filled kids' bath, our special design issue is sure to give you a head start.

An array of beautiful products in outstanding settings awaits you!

*Laura Kohler*

LAURA E. KOHLER
*Director, Public Affairs*

Project Editor: Heather J. Paper; Art Director: Jody Tramontina; Design Director: Jann Williams; Managing Editor: Deb Gore Ohrn; Editor-in-Chief: Don Johnson; Production: Ivan McDonald; Marketing Director: Christopher W. Schraft; Publisher: Joe Mangione.

# table of contents

COVER

*This bathroom features above-counter lavatories that take the everyday ritual of washing to a new level. See page 26.*

# partner profiles

The relationships formed between Kohler Co. and its multiple partners are important to the success of the team as a whole. And that success is to your advantage; it translates to well-coordinated, high-style products for your kitchen and bath. Here's what Kohler Co. and its various partners have to offer.

### KOHLER CO.

plumbing products are world-renowned, having come a long way since 1873, when John Michael Kohler took a horse trough, heated it up to 1700 degrees, and sprinkled on some enamel powder. He liked it so much that he offered it in a catalog, noting that, "when fitted with four legs, the unit could serve as a bathtub."

Through the years, Kohler's dedication to excellence has forged one of the oldest and largest privately held companies in the United States, a company that has grown to international stature with over 17,000 associates worldwide.

### ROBERN

specializes in the design and manufacture of mirrored bath cabinetry and lighting for the home. From an elegant single-door cabinet to a lavatory wall complete with multiple storage units, lighting, accessories, and lavs, Robern products are found in the finest baths.

### CANAC

cabinetry, made since 1966, isn't just for the kitchen and bath. Offering more than 50 cabinet styles and 400 door color and finish combinations, this cabinetry is just as appropriate for built-ins in the library, laundry, pantry, bedroom, and bar.

ANN SACKS TILE AND STONE
has come a long way since Ann Sacks
began her operation with three tiles she
carried in a shoe box on rounds to potential customers. The company now main-
tains eight showrooms, operates two manufacturing facilities in the Pacific
Northwest, and imports tile, marble, granite, and limestone from ten countries.

SUB-ZERO,
the ultimate name in refrigeration, pioneered the
concept of built-ins. Today it's taking that innovation
one step further with integrated models that allow you
to place the refrigerator or freezer anywhere you'd put
a cabinet or drawer.

DUTCH BOY PAINT
has, for 90 years, been the most
trusted brand for those people
who want to paint their "American
dream." Its thousands of colors are
tested-tough and guaranteed to
give your home a great paint job
with long-lasting beauty.

WILSONART INTERNATIONAL
brings you smart surfacing materials with a diverse
line of high-quality products. With Wilsonart, you
can create unique solutions for countertops,
decorative edgings, walls, tub and shower surrounds,
backsplashes, and even flooring.

DALTILE
is dedicated to providing
innovative tile with
unrivaled consistency,
quality, and availability.
Offering a vast product
selection—and well-
trained professional
consultants—Daltile is
poised to become your
single source for tile.

DACOR
appliances take the art of
cooking to a new level. The
award-winning designs are
matched only by superior
performance. Whether
you're preparing a "solo"
meal or orchestrating food
for a crowd, Dacor offers a
range of possibilities.

# kohler color

There's no doubt about it—coordinating elements in a room can be as confusing as a jigsaw puzzle. But Kohler and its partner companies have put the pieces together for you. The Kohler Coordinates program does the mixing and matching, letting you know which elements work well together. For clues about the hottest new color combinations, look for exciting "Kohler schemes" throughout the publication.

HISTORICALLY, KOHLER'S COLOR palette has been known for its boldness and influence in the industry. And throughout time, the so-called color "white" has challenged those efforts. Today, that challenge is greater than ever before—for a lot of reasons—but primarily because of the popularity of traditional design in plumbing products.

That's not to say that white isn't still a perfectly valid choice; it's simply that there's a brave—and colorful—new world out there. And Kohler Co., with its select team

of partners, has set out to prove just how comfortable it can be to live in color.

We're not talking trendy colors here. Rather, the search is for shades that will have longevity. And we're not talking about color for color's sake either, but as a way to enhance the product itself. In fact, Kohler Co.'s new Vessels™ are a perfect example. The lavatories' textural matte glazes make the simple elegance of the shapes even more pronounced.

In the Kohler palette, you'll find dramatic blacks, hunter greens, and icy blues—all of which work so well with other colors that they're neutrals in their own right.

If, however, you'd like to proceed more slowly to add color to your bath, there's a simple solution. The "Story of Stone" is one of Kohler's

ABOVE: **The decorative aspect of these twin sinks is carried out with complementary tile.**
LEFT: **The "Story of Stone" is an important part of Kohler's new color palette, including shades influenced by Mother Nature's own elements.**
RIGHT: **Taking color to the limit, this assortment of products is evidence of the brave new world of color that's out there!**

first steps toward swinging the pendulum away from pure white. Influenced by wood and stone as well as various metals and glass, this group of handsome fixtures creates spaces that intrinsically feel good. Some of Kohler Co.'s new introductions include:

■ White Cliffs, a cool-white, lightly speckled finish with blue-green and gray flecks, is reminiscent of the legendary white-chalk Cliffs of Dover.

■ Stoneware, a warm-white, lightly speckled finish with brown and black flecks, creates a feeling much like stoneware pottery.

■ Cream City, an even warmer shade of white highlighted with brown and black flecks evokes the feeling of traditional architectural bricks from the Midwest.

And what can you expect of color in the kitchen? Something just a little more daring, that's what. One of the hottest hues is Iron Cobalt, also with mineral origins. Enameled onto a cast-iron sink, for instance, the result is both bold and beautiful. And don't be afraid to make the most of it—right up to and including making it the room's focal point.

In short, don't be afraid to splash color throughout your kitchen and bath. You're bound to find the results rewarding, from a visual perspective and from a psychological one, as well.

# what's new and
notable

For Kohler Co. and its partners, innovation doesn't stop with the color palette. Every aspect of their respective lines is functionally fit and aesthetically friendly. So, take a minute to peruse these new products. You'll be impressed with these high-tech, soft-touch introductions.

ABOVE: **From Ann Sacks Tile and Stone, these decorative tiles have that comfortable, been-loved-for-years look.**
RIGHT: **This cobalt blue basin, from Kohler Co., starts every morning with a wake-up call!**
BOTTOM RIGHT: **Within this Canac cabinetry, polyester and wood doors have been cleverly mixed for a French country look. Varied counter heights provide even more eye-catching interest.**
OPPOSITE: **These mirrored bath cabinets by Robern, with a floating glass lav, create a focal point while occupying little visual space.**

ABOVE: **Interior Cabinet and Trim Paint from Dutch Boy Paint is tough enough to withstand the beating that cabinets and trim take every day.**
TOP RIGHT: **The 700 Series by Sub-Zero allows you to have refrigerator service anywhere you would normally put a door or drawer.**
RIGHT: **From Daltile, Gold Rush™ ceramic flooring is softly colored and hard-working at the same time, while complementary wall and decorative tiles complete the look.**

# what's new and
## notable

LEFT: **Laminate flooring from Wilsonart offers the best of all worlds in your kitchen—the beauty of hardwoods with even more durability.**

BELOW LEFT: **From Dacor, this slide-in range offers cooking versatility with duel fuel—a self-cleaning convection electric oven and four 15000 BTU sealed-gas burners.**

BELOW: **The Finial Art™ faucet set by Kohler Co. features easy-to-grip lever handles enhanced with a distinct decorative flair.**

# ask the expert

An expert isn't always on call when you need one. But on these two pages, we're offering the next best thing. Karol DeWulf Nickell, Editor-in-Chief of *Traditional Home* magazine, takes time to answer a few of our readers' most oft-asked questions. Her expertise may just provide the solution to a problem that you've been pondering!

ABOVE:

**Editor-in-Chief of *Traditional Home* magazine, Karol DeWulf Nickell**

q I SELECTED A PAINT COLOR FOR MY bathroom based on a paint chip. But now that it's on my walls, the color looks too bright. What can I do to prevent this from happening again?

a The best test of a color's effect is to buy a small amount of that paint, brush it on a two-foot-square piece of paper, and hang the paper in the room you plan to paint. Live with it for a few days to see how it feels; many times, you'll find that a less intense shade will be a better choice.

While you're evaluating your hues, keep in mind, too, that fluorescent and incandescent lights affect colors. Fluorescent lighting cools colors, giving them a bluish cast. Incandescent lighting, on the other hand, warms them. To best showcase your colors of choice, use full-spectrum lighting.

q I'M IN THE PROCESS OF REMODELING my kitchen, but all of the sinks I've seen are too conventional—or contemporary—for the vintage look I'm trying to achieve. Is there something that will give me the ambience I'm searching for?

a Suitable for the most simple cottage-style kitchen or a sophisticated traditional environment, an apron-front sink like the one shown *below* imparts vintage charm. According to your tastes—and the mood of the room—you may choose a plain, all-white model, much like you'd have found in your grandmother's kitchen. Or, make a more decorative statement with a beautifully embossed style.

Like a room without the proper accessories, though, a sink isn't complete without the proper faucets and fittings. These, too, can greatly influence the final effect. From the most understated farmhouse look to an archetypal appearance, there's a wealth of ways to create a classic attitude.

THE SMALL DIMENSIONS OF MY kitchen make it necessary to use every inch to the maximum. At the same time, though, my husband and I entertain extensively. How can I accommodate all of our needs within such a limited space?

You'll be surprised at how many amenities you can incorporate into a well-planned kitchen. Use the one at *right*, for instance, for inspiration. White base cabinets provide plenty of storage while—from a visual point of view—blending quietly into the background. (There's even an under-counter refrigerator tucked away for extra cold-storage space.) And above, wall-hung storage units take the concept to another level; glass-fronted cabinets seemingly recede even further into the room while housing a decorative collection of dinnerware.

A closer look at this kitchen reveals even more features for entertaining. Set into one end of the counter, a sink accommodates food preparation on a day-to-day basis yet serves up bar needs when guests arrive. Plus, a work island can be transformed into an informal buffet!

I'D LIKE TO USE CERAMIC TILE ON THE floor in my preschooler's bathroom, but I'm afraid it will be hard to keep clean and too slippery for a toddler. What are my options?

Ceramic tile would be an excellent choice for a child's bathroom. And with accent tiles in bright primary colors, it promises to be a visually appealing one, too. (Keep your eye out, too, for tiles that are pre-coordinated with many of today's fixtures.)

Regarding your concern about clean-up, it couldn't be easier. For the most part, a simple damp mopping is all that's needed. As for safety, it's a matter of smart shopping. Some tiles are more slip-resistant than others; check with your retailer for the most appropriate choices.

I'VE BEEN NOTICING A MORE EXTENsive use of fine furniture in the bath. Is it really safe to use treasured pieces in such a high-humidity area?

Chosen carefully, fine wood furnishings can be incorporated into a bath like the one at *right*. Placement is important, though; nothing should be positioned too close to a water source. But there is an exception to the rule; beautiful vanities are being built to accommodate lavatories. You might even use wash-and-wear terry toweling as slipcovers for chairs!

MY HUSBAND AND I ARE FINALLY adding a bathroom. What are the basics we should know?

Your current plumbing system will influence where your new bath fixtures can be placed. Be sure to take this present system into account; it's less expensive to drain into the existing stack.

For a basic remodeling, you should be able to do much of the preliminary work yourselves. If your remodeling involves structural, electrical, or plumbing changes, consider hiring a professional.

Luxurious

Invigorating

Peaceful

Jump-Starting

Romantic

Beautiful

Hardworking

Meditative

Refreshing

Personal

Relaxing

Private

Energizing

Pampering

Soothing

Sumptuous

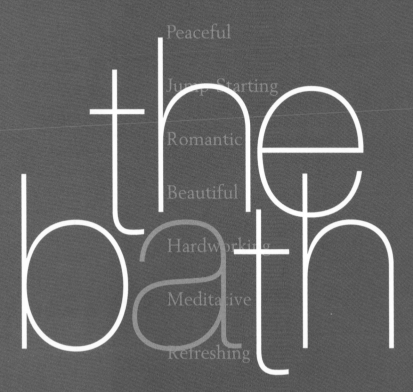

the bath

# the master bath

It wasn't until the 18th century that the bath became a private sanctuary. And since then, it's only become a more coveted retreat. The master bath, in particular, has become a place for pure pampering—to rev up at the day's start and to wind down at day's end. And here's the best news: It's as good for the body as it is for the soul.

A LUXURIOUS MASTER BATH IS ONE OF the most highly regarded amenities in today's home. But make no mistake: It needn't be big to be beautiful. Baths of all sizes can be spa-like in their attitude.

To plan the perfect master bath, start by thinking about your basic needs. Do you like to soak in the tub…or is a quick shower more your style? And what else is on your list of necessities? A single sink or twin bowls? A toilet as well as a bidet? Only after you've made definite decisions about the essentials can you go on to consider more personal pleasures.

And what is it, exactly, that turns a simple bathroom into a bathing beauty? That depends on your point of view. If you're an English-country enthusiast, it may be treasured collectibles in every corner of the room. Or if clean-lined contemporary is your preference, uncluttered expanses of gleaming tile may be more to your liking.

Maybe you're not even sure what specific style you want to adopt. If that's the case, close your eyes for a moment and think about the most luxurious master bath you've ever seen. Whether it was in the home of a friend or a five-star hotel, chances are—if it made a good first impression—it's a look you'll feel comfortable with for years to come. Don't be afraid to indulge yourself on a daily basis.

OPPOSITE: **At a time when master baths rival the sizes of their accompanying bedrooms, sumptuous style is the order of the day. In this luxurious bath, for instance, a grand illusion is established as much by the room's dimensions as it is by the overall design.**
LEFT: **There's no "jumping in and out" of this shower. The sheer size— easily large enough for two—makes you want to linger longer.**

# working with the pros

BATHS, WITH THEIR INHERENT PLUMBING
requirements, often call for professional help. But before you team up
with a pro, you should know what to
expect from him or her.

Decide first whether you'll work
with an interior designer, a certified
bathroom designer (CBD), or plumbing contractor. Whomever you
choose should be able to assess your
needs, offer specific suggestions, and
recommend products that will meet
your needs.

Last but not least, a professional
should be able to help you stay within your personal budget and steer
you toward the best choices for your
design dollars.

LEFT: **Given the advantage of an extra-high ceiling, the designer of this contemporary bath created a bi-level design. The result? The owners step up and into the tub, lending the space a worlds-away ambience that's restful and relaxing.**

OPPOSITE: **The designer of this master bath was inspired by a Toulouse-Lautrec print, which gives the room a certain French flair. Fine furnishings, such as the sink-side lamp and a gold-upholstered armchair, make this master bath as design-conscious as any other room in the house.**

LONG PAST THE TIME WHEN IT SERVED a purely utilitarian purpose, the bath now sports as much style as any other room in the house. In fact, because it's such a private sanctuary, you can indulge your personal preferences to the hilt.

Go beyond conventional trappings and add a comfortable chair, chaise, or even a window seat. You may be surprised how relaxing it can be to curl up in a robe and read a few pages of a favorite book. Or, if you're a traditionalist, search out antiques to soften the hard-edge look of bath fixtures. You can even add art and collectibles, as shown here.

A word to the wise, however: When placing fine art or furniture in a bathroom, make sure it can stand up to the inevitable moisture.

personal
pursuits

pamper *yourself*

THINK ABOUT IT FOR JUST A MOMENT. What makes you feel pampered? Maybe it's soaking in an oversize bathtub beneath a star-studded skylight. Or perhaps it's something as simple as a bath-side bookshelf or telephone. From sweet-smelling bath oils and thick, thirsty towels to built-in saunas and spas—the sky's the limit in terms of what you can add to your master bath for that purely pampering experience.

And with today's yen for healthy bodies, don't forget to include fitness and audiovisual equipment. Those amenities, plus a comfortable after-exercise sitting spot, are sure to add up to a space that even the ancient Romans would envy.

ABOVE: **Why, after a soothing bath, should you have to pad all the way to another room to curl up with a book? Tuck a chaise into a corner, then add a wall of built-in bookshelves nearby.**
LEFT: **As the room's focal point, this tub commands a great deal of importance— making the bather feel important, too. Rich color throughout adds a sense of luxury.**

storage
solutions

MIRRORED BATH CABINETS ARE STANDARD in many a bathroom. With extra deep options and interior electrical outs, they're more efficient than ever. But what if you need even more storage space…and are looking for something a little less conventional?

■ Take a tip from kitchen design and incorporate an island. Doors and drawers in a variety of sizes can discreetly conceal towels and toiletries.

■ Move a favorite chest into the bathroom for storage with style.

■ A wall of built-in shelving is perfect for towels, soaps and lotions, and even books.

■ Don't forget simple everyday items. Wicker baskets can provide portable storage for magazines and towels, and apothecary jars are perfect for smaller essentials.

LEFT: **Today's mirrored bath cabinets, like this one from Robern, are roomier. Thus, they can hold much more than medicine!**

OPPOSITE: **The curved backdrop for this pedestal sink is more than merely aesthetic; there's drawer storage built into both sides and open shelves on the right.**

THE SELECTION OF COUNTER MATERIALS
has never been more impressive.
Depending on your preference, any
one of the following can make a
splash in your bath.

*Laminate* is a popular material for
two key reasons: It's inexpensive and
it comes in assorted colors and patterns. Made from a $\frac{1}{16}$-inch sandwich
of paper and resin bonded to $\frac{3}{4}$-inch
plywood or particleboard, laminate
resists soaps, stains, and hot water.
And, it can be customized in myriad
ways with a wide variety of edgings.

*Solid-surfacing* is more expensive
than laminate, but its beauty and
durability make it well worth the
price. (As an intermediate option,
there are *solid-surfacing veneers* that
offer the look and performance of
solid-surface materials at a much
lower price.) The thickness of the
material makes it difficult to damage,
and the nonporous surface keeps
germs and dirt at bay, resisting mold
and stains. Custom decorative treatments include insets, heat-molded
edge designs, and integrated sinks.

*Glazed ceramic tile* offers limitless
colors and patterns—as do the wide
variety of borders and edge treatments. And, thanks to its fired-clay
makeup, tile is almost as tough as
stone, offering the ultimate in stain
resistance. It can withstand heat,
moisture, and even chemicals.

# counter
## revolution

LEFT: **From solid-color squares to decorative edgings, ceramic tile enables endless design options. In this master bath, simple black and white tiles showcase their versatility; they're not only used on the counter but also on the wall, the floor, even the tub surround.**

OPPOSITE: **Not only are solid-surface materials available in pastel hues, they're also great pretenders. Marble and granite look-alikes—like this example from Wilsonart—can give you the same sophisticated style at a price that's easier on the budget.**

# making a splash

IF YOU THINK ALL SINKS ARE CREATED EQUAL, THINK AGAIN. PEDESTAL SINKS AND

Vessels™ are decorative options, but even more common countertop sinks come in a wide variety of styles.

The most popular sink, the countertop, is a self-rimming sink that sits atop the counter; a rim simply overlaps the cutout, providing support for the sink itself. Conversely, under-mount sinks are installed from beneath, allowing the countertop to extend over the sink's edges. The result is a contemporary look that perhaps best complements solid-surface surrounds, but also works with tile and stone. And there are even flush-mounted sinks with squared edges that allow installation flush with a ceramic-tile countertop. As for integral basins, they're simply made of the same material as the countertop itself, usually a solid-surface material.

An alternative to the conventional countertop sink is the fashion-minded Vessel. Set atop the counter, a Vessel is a contemporary option that's as attractive as it is utilitarian.

And what if space is at a premium? In a powder room or a similarly small bath, freestanding pedestal sinks are a particularly good choice.

RIGHT: **Decorative in its design, these above-counter lavatories take the everyday ritual of washing to a new level. The fittings can be as artistic as the Vessel itself.**

LEFT: **Start with a decorative pedestal sink to create a focal point in your master bath. Then take your color cues from it to build a palette for the entire room.**

what's the
difference?

A LONG HOT BATH AT THE END OF THE
day is one of the most popular ways
to unwind. But what type of tub best
suits you and your lifestyle?

The size and shape of your bathtub will depend much on your available space, how you plan to use the
tub and, of course, aesthetics. Many
bathtubs now incorporate gentle
curves, sloping backs, pillows, and
armrests to make for a more comfortable bathing experience.

If you'd like to share your soak,
round, oval, and hourglass shapes are
perfect for two. And, at the opposite
end of the spectrum, space-saving
square and triangular baths are
designed to tuck neatly into corners.

OPPOSITE:**A copper
tub from Kohler's
Kallista collection
nestled into a bump-
out area is given
a regal draping of
sheer fabric hung
from an antique
French canopy
crown. A fireplace
and easy chair
add to the relaxing
experience.**
LEFT: **Surrounded by
glass, this two-per-
son whirlpool tub is
a haven by daylight
or moonlight, creat-
ing a spot with an
unmistakably "pam-
per-me" attitude.**

# what's the difference?

IT USED TO BE A TEN-MINUTE RITUAL. BUT
today's showers tempt you to stand
in them for hours. Pulsating body
sprays, soft mist, therapeutic steam—
these are just a few of the options on
the latest enclosures.

To accommodate these options,
your shower should be larger than
the standard 32- or 36-inch square
one. There's no limit to the number
of showerheads you can install. And
the ultimate? Without a doubt, it's
the luxurious 10-jet BodySpa™.

If, however, you're trying to use
your space more efficiently, consider
one of the new neo-angle showers.
They're comprised of a glass door
and two glass panels you can set next
to tile, marble, or granite walls or a
prefab corner unit. The base can be
angled or partially rounded, extend-
ing from 36 to 72 inches along the
two walls, and the doors can be clear,
frosted, etched, or thick-tempered
glass. With these neo-angle showers,
you simply add the sprays and showerheads of your choice.

RIGHT: **The equiva-
lent of a "vertical
whirlpool," this
10-jet BodySpa by
Kohler is the epito-
me of luxury. The
perfect workout
after exercise, it
targets body-level
jets and head/neck
jets toward tired,
aching muscles.**
LEFT: **The utmost
in space-saving
convenience, this
neo-angle shower
is a simple, straight-
forward design.**

soothing schemes

FOR SOME, THE IDYLLIC MASTER BATH IS A PLACE TO SOAK YOUR CARES AWAY AT THE
end of a long day. But a deep whirlpool, bath oils, and beads—even some
aromatherapy—are only part of the equation. Color can play a large role
in the overall effect, creating a mood that's as soothing as the bathing
experience itself.

Neutral hues in particular can induce this kind of feeling. Pale colors can
fade away into nothingness, equating a quiet solitude. That's not to say that
this kind of space is bland or boring. Instead, a variety of textures can keep
things interesting—from the sleek glass sur-
faces to rough-hewn wood to subtly sponged
paint on the walls. In addition, it's easy to
infuse a splash of color in an understated
space by simply changing and rearranging your
favorite accessories.

OPPOSITE: **To double
the drama of this
master bath, a cus-
tom mirror reflects
the intricate shape
of the vanity below.
It also serves a
more practical pur-
pose by bouncing
light around the
room.**
LEFT: **Surrounding
the bathtub, the
graceful shapes
established by the
mirror and vanity
are repeated—this
time in paint—at
ceiling level.**

RIGHT: **Taking a cue from Mother Nature, this seafoam-green bath gives you the feeling of floating upon a sea of calm. To emphasize the effect, a corner tub gets a grand view of the water beyond.**
OPPOSITE: **It's a space you could be hard-pressed to want to leave. Beyond the basics, this master bath is outfitted with open shelving—for everything from trunks to a television—as well as a writing table and a terry-covered chair.**

By taking advantage of color's mood-setting talents, your master bath can convey a very personal message. But it's up to you to decide which colors will best get that message across.

To some, for instance, red may prove to be energizing; to others, it's nothing less than nerve-racking. Likewise, some people see blues and greens as cool and calming, even though some shades can be positively electrifying. So consider the possibilities. What color are you most comfortable with?

## WHAT'S YOUR TEMPERATURE?

Nature sets the color thermostat, so it's important to consider the visual temperature of the hues in your master-bath palette. The spectrum's cooler side—including blues, greens, and violets—fosters introspection and calm. Bright, warm hues, on the other hand—reds, yellows, and oranges—can buoy the spirits and produce a fun-loving room, regardless of your decorating style.

color your world

# tiletalk

THERE'S A REASON YOU SEE CERAMIC TILE IN
so many bathrooms: Its long list of
advantages makes tile attractive for
more than aesthetic reasons. Beyond
the limitless colors, patterns, and textures, ceramic tile is durable and
affordable. And, this easy-to-clean
option is impervious to water and
most other liquids.

There's a bevy of beautiful tiles on
the market today—many of them
custom designs that are meticulously
handmade. If you're keeping close
watch on your budget, though, select
a less-expensive field tile and splurge
on trim tiles. For instance, you can
cap tile that rises halfway up the wall
with a "pencil" molding or bas-relief
tiles in a matching color to achieve a
strong architectural look.

RIGHT: **Not only is tile a practical choice
for this whirlpool surround, it also gives
the bathing spot a certain status. In this
neutral room, the texture of the tile adds
visual variety and, in fact, makes the area
an eye-catching focal point.**

RIGHT: **As proven
by the chair
rail effect in this
bath, decorative
tiles can add
real excitement
to a room.**
OPPOSITE: **To make
sure you'll have no
regrets later about a
colorful tile design,
take a tip from this
master bath with its
ocher, green, and
raspberry tiles. Use
graph paper and
colored pencils to
sketch different
pattern possibilities
to scale.**

tiletalk

If you're planning to use ceramic tile in your master bath, keep in mind that selecting the tile itself is only the first step. The grout you choose also will have a big impact on the final results.

When selecting a grout color, first consider whether you want your project to look monochromatic or whether you'd like to accentuate the tile color and texture. You'll need to use a grout color similar to your tile to create a uniform-looking installation; contrasting grout will highlight each tile and create a gridlike pattern.

Keep in mind, too, that portland-cement-based grouts come in sanded and nonsanded versions. *Sanded* grouts are used with floor tiles and when the grout joint is wider than $\frac{1}{8}$ inch. *Nonsanded* grouts, on the other hand, are used for joints narrower than $\frac{1}{8}$ inch or when the tile glaze could be scratched by sanded grout.

Finally, plan the width of grout joints based on the type of tile—and on the look you want. Porcelain tiles are cut precisely, so joints can be minimal, but irregular handmade tiles may need joints wider than $\frac{1}{2}$ inch.

on the
wall

FACE IT: THE WALL TREATMENTS IN YOUR bath have to be more than pretty faces. They also have to withstand plenty of moisture.

For tub and shower surrounds, pick something waterproof such as a solid-surface material. Ceramic tile is a good choice, too, plus it's a great way to bring color and texture to the adjacent walls. Marble and limestone tile are glamorous, too. You should think twice before using these materials on counters (they're prone to stains) but you shouldn't have any trouble using them on walls.

Finally, paint and wall coverings can work well in areas that won't be splashed with water. Stick with easy-to-clean options, however, such as scrubbable, high-sheen paint or vinyl-coated wall coverings.

LEFT: **Start every day with a little sunshine by painting bathroom walls a bright yellow. Then, take a cue from this bath and add bright accents to drive home the cheery ambience.**

TOP RIGHT: **Wallpapers like this green-and-white pinstripe can add instant color and pattern to a room. For easy clean-up, though, make sure they're vinyl-coated.**

BOTTOM RIGHT: **If you're looking for a waterproof shower surround, consider a solid-surface option like this one from Wilsonart.**

# floor
## shows

GIVEN THE VAST EXPANSE OF THE FLOOR, IT can—and should—be treated just as decoratively as a wall. Your choice of material will depend on your budget, of course, as well as your personal preferences, but ceramic stone, wood, tile, and laminate are four of the most stylish possibilities.

Whichever you choose, don't overlook safety, though. Glossy tiles may be beautiful, but they're also easy to slip on. Instead, you might opt for slip-resistant tiles that have a matte or textured finish.

# the right light

To make your master bath as inviting as any other room in the house, you'll want to avoid harsh, utilitarian lighting. Instead, choose a mixture of fixtures to give the room a little atmosphere.

For general lighting, multiple recessed ceiling fixtures look and perform better than a single ceiling-mounted fixture. You'll want to place at least two above the vanity; above the tub and shower, install a recessed fixture designed specifically for damp areas.

Additionally, consider sconces that bounce light off the ceiling. You might flank the vanity mirror with a pair of decorative sconces with glass globes. Incandescent or fluorescent tubes—even multi-bulb theatrical strips—would work just as well.

Last, but not least, carefully consider task lighting. Good illumination is imperative to tasks such as applying makeup and shaving.

OPPOSITE: **Although halogen, fluorescent, and incandescent lighting all are important to a room, don't neglect your most inexpensive source—natural light. When it comes to providing comfortable light, it's unequaled.**
LEFT: **Positioned equidistantly along the vanity mirror, linear lights are just the thing for beauty and grooming tasks.**

# the family bath

Because it's used by all members of the family, the family bath is—without a doubt—the biggest design challenge. It has to serve the short and the tall, the old and the young, those who are in and out in a flash, and those who prefer to linger. There's good news, though: It can do all this and more—and do it beautifully.

As OPPOSED TO MAKING DECISIONS single-handedly, planning a family bath is more like bringing each issue before a board of directors. It's not always easy to plan a family bath that will make everyone perfectly happy. So, how best to achieve harmony? Start—as you would with any other room in the house—by doing some careful planning. Beyond the requisite plumbing, for instance, how do you want your bathroom to feel and function? Would twin sinks ease the family's morning rush hour? Does a lounging spot, exercise space, hot tub, or laundry nook top your list of luxuries?

Likewise, what mood do you want to convey? A swath of fresh color, a vintage-style fixture, a sleek tile floor—even eye-catching art and collectibles—can make a big splash.

Finally, after you've allowed for function and ambience, think about how each member of the family will use the bath. If you have small children in the family, it's important that they be able to reach their daily "essentials" (toothbrush, toothpaste, etc.) but not be able to access dangerous medicines (see "Safety First" on *pages 50-51*). And if you have seniors or family members with disabilities, products such as grab bars, barrier-free tubs and showers, and non-slip tile take on even more importance.

With a little planning, you can accommodate everyone while creating the perfect look to greet you in the morning and soothe you at night—and keep peace in the family at the same time.

OPPOSITE: **Given sufficient space, it's wise to divide a family bath into separate stations. That way, more than one person can use the room—putting less pressure on the morning rush hour.**

a place for everything

YOU SIMPLY CAN'T HAVE TOO MUCH STORAGE, so think beyond the conventional and find ways to incorporate favorite things into every nook and cranny.

In this dramatic black-and-white bathroom, a mirrored bath cabinet and open-shelved linen closet play out traditional roles. But it's the room's nooks and niches that make the subtle difference. Beneath the bath cabinet, a glass shelf is a convenient spot for a makeup mirror and other small essentials. Meanwhile, over the bathtub, an arched setback becomes the perfect place for shampoos and scrubbing brushes. Even the ledge beneath the window serves as a prominent display for treasured collectibles.

RIGHT: **For safety and luxury at the same time, this whirlpool features grab bars and, in the back and shoulder areas, ten pulsating jets creating the feeling of a soothing massage.**

OPPOSITE: **Installing a mirrored bath cabinet like this is one of the best safety measures you can take. It's outfitted with a lockable flip-up door.**

safety first

FAR TOO OFTEN, WE HEAR ABOUT ACCIDENTS happening in the bathroom. An inquisitive child inadvertently takes a prescription medication. Someone slips on a slick tile surface. Elderly family members fall when getting in or out of the bathtub.

The good news is that advances are being made every day to prevent these accidents and injuries. Here are a few of the latest:

■ Mirrored bath cabinets now are available with lock boxes.

■ Grip rails can be added to some bathtubs and whirlpools, making it easier to get in and out. Likewise, you can also install grab bars next to bathtubs, showers, and toilets.

■ Today's nonslip varieties of tile are less slippery underfoot when there's water splashed around on the bathroom floor. They offer all the beauty of tile floors with less danger of falling.

# the guest bath

Your guest bath should be more than an any-old-thing-will-do room. Instead, design it as if it were for your best friend. If you're not sure where to start, use this simple rule: Include everything that *you'd* like to find when staying at a hotel or visiting a friend's home. Then, to make sure it really works, try it out yourself.

LIKE A GUEST BEDROOM, THE GUEST bath presents virtually limitless decorating options. It's here that you can be a gracious host or hostess, providing your guests everything you'd like to find yourself as an overnight visitor. It's here where you can put finishing touches on the warmest of welcomes.

In fact, *planning* a guest bath can be half the fun! As you visit friends and relatives, take note of what niceties they include in their guest baths. And when you stay at a hotel or resort, note which little extras make you feel particularly pampered.

But, as the saying goes, don't miss the forest for the trees. As important as the fragrant soaps and thick towels are, fixtures still come first. The guest bath may be smaller than its master counterpart, but that doesn't mean it has to be any less dramatic. Why not select a stunning pedestal sink to serve as a focal point? Or, you might settle on a simple soaking tub and give it a place of prominence in front of a bay window. Another option is a unique shower. These kinds of choices will

make your guests feel like they're truly someplace special.

There's even a bonus to making your guest bath so inviting: Your guests will want to return often. And there's no reason you can't use it yourself once in a while, too.

OPPOSITE: **Floating cabinets and a tri-fold mirror team up to create the illusion of space in this guest bath. The room's dramatic decor makes guests feel extra special.**
LEFT: **For a truly relaxing experience, this shower features hydromassage and a standard shower in the same unit. Your guests may not want to ever leave!**

To PLAY THE PART OF THE PERFECT HOST OR hostess, start by putting yourself in the role of the invited guest. When it comes to a luxurious bath, what's on your wish list? Maybe it's something as simple as a cup of tea and an interesting selection of books and magazines waiting at bathside. On the other hand, don't be afraid to think big. Perhaps nothing short of a whirlpool or a private dressing table makes you feel pampered.

To get started planning your own guest bath, here are a few simple accessories to consider:

- Plenty of thick, thirsty towels
- A basket full of assorted soaps, shampoos, conditioners, and creams
- An extra terry-cloth robe or two
- Scented candles that can be lit during a luxurious bath
- A few stems of fresh flowers
- A hair dryer, toothbrush, toothpaste, and any other incidentals your guest may have forgotten
- Essentials, including facial tissues, cotton balls, and a wastebasket.

Finally, step back and admire the retreat you've created. How do you know if it will be a success? Take a day to be a guest in your own home and you'll quickly find out!

RIGHT: **The library look is invariably cozy and comfortable, so why not extend it into the bathroom? This example is complete with built-in bookshelves, favorite prints, and formal lighting fixtures.**

TOP LEFT: **Given a multitude of amenities, this guest bath is well-thought-out down to the last detail, including beautiful Accentials™ tile from Daltile.**

BOTTOM LEFT: **To pamper your guests, give them a dressing table to call their own. There's something purely luxurious about having the time and space to sit down and "primp."**

be my
guest

easy *does it*

THOUGH GUEST BATHS, BY NATURE, DON'T get used on a day-to-day basis, you should still make the surfaces easy to clean. When choosing surface materials for your bathroom floors, walls, and countertops, think about what it will take to keep them looking new.

*Decorative laminate* should be wiped with a solution of mild liquid cleaner or nonabrasive cleaner. To remove stubborn spills, let the cleaner set awhile to loosen the material.

*Solid-surface materials* require an abrasive cleaner to maintain surface luster. To remove burns and scratches, lightly sand with fine sandpaper according to the manufacturer's recommendations.

*Washable wallpaper* needs only a damp cloth and a little mild soap to wipe off most soil.

*Tile*, too, is easy-care, requiring only a damp cloth and a mild cleanser.

*Paint*, especially in semi- and high-gloss finishes, is easy to clean with nothing more than a damp cloth.

*Wood* should be dusted with a soft cloth and cleaned with a mild, non-alkaline soap and water.

LEFT: **The fixtures and furnishings in this bath reflect the room's avant-garde design. Intentionally kept simple, the wall-hung sink and nearby round table allow the decorative tile to be the star.**

LIKE ANY OTHER ROOM IN THE HOUSE, YOUR guest bath should make a personal style statement. If you favor Queen Anne furnishings, for instance, make sure that your bath reflects your traditional tendencies. Likewise, if Bauhaus is the theme at your house, keep your guest bath as contemporary as the rest of your residence. By putting your personality into the room, not only will you appreciate it more, but your visitors will gain some insight into your style predilections, too!

## SUITE SENSATIONS

Even if you don't have the luxury of a guest suite, you can create a similar feeling by giving small spaces the suite treatment. You might give both the bedroom and bath the same decorative paint treatment. Or, reverse the colors and patterns you use in the two rooms.

OPPOSITE: **The soothing neutral colors are only part of the reason guests linger in this room. The traditional trimmings invite them to relax for hours.**
BELOW: **With its row of high windows and hardwareless cabinetry, this contemporary bath lends itself to the geometric blue-check walls. Because the pattern provides so much pizzazz, very few accessories are required—just a piece of pottery and a favorite print.**

style
statements

# the powder room

It may have diminutive dimensions, but that's no reason to sell it short. In fact, the powder room presents a wonderful opportunity to make a great first impression! Treat it as a gift for your guests, all wrapped up in eye-catching colors and patterns. Then, in place of ribbons and bows, give your tiny treasure the perfect finishing touches!

MANY PEOPLE TAKE ONE LOOK AT their powder rooms and all but throw up their hands in despair. "What," they think, "can you possibly do with such a small space?"

In fact, there's plenty you can do with this special room. But first you need the right mind-set. Think of the powder room as a diamond in the rough, a gem waiting to be polished. It may not appear to be much at first, but the results can be dazzling!

You can create your own little jewel any number of ways. For example, even basic bath fixtures can assume star status. Start by choosing a sink and toilet in a smashing color or an unusual style. Then go a step further and select extra-special faucets and fittings.

Surfaces, too, can make any number of style statements. Decorative laminate, solid-surface materials, ceramic tile, and natural stone all can create stunning countertops. Or take an even more artful approach and incorporate fine wood furniture such as a traditional vanity predrilled for a basin and wide-set faucets.

As for the walls, the possibilities are just as plentiful. Ceramic tile, innovative wall coverings, and paint in every color of the rainbow can effect styles from strictly contemporary to lavishly traditional. Especially, consider paint for its decorative potential. Sponging, combing, ragging, glazing, and *trompe l'oeil* (three-dimensional murals) are techniques whose results are particularly impressive when showcased in such a small space.

OPPOSITE: **Skirted in gauzy fabric, this sink is dressed up and ready to receive guests. Upholstered walls in a French-inspired toile and an old Irish chest (used to store linens) give the room old-world ambience.**

BELOW: **Decorative powder-room fixtures add instant drama. This lavatory by Kohler—decked out in peonies and ivy—was inspired by Victorian floral imagery.**

TO EXPAND THE SPACE IN YOUR POWDER ROOM—AT LEAST VISUALLY—TURN TO ONE
of the most effective tricks of the trade. Mirrors can make the most of
areas with even the smallest square footage.

You might want to mirror one entire wall to double your dimensions.
But smaller mirrors are effective, too. Consider hanging a beautifully
framed mirror over a pedestal sink; a graceful oval shape, especially, can
soften hard-edge fixtures. And don't forget, mirrored bath cabinets come
in all shapes and sizes, ready to keep necessities close at hand.

Finally, think about using mirrors in a purely decorative manner. In lieu
of grouping small prints in a prominent spot, arrange a collection of small
mirrors. Complemented by frames in the style of your choice, they'll
instantly reflect the mood of your room.

RIGHT: **This assem-
blage of five mir-
rored cabinets,
halogen lights, and
an integral all-glass
lav is inarguably the
focal point of this
powder room. The
larger-than-usual
cabinet visually
adds square footage
to the room, too.**
LEFT: **Because the
glass lav "floats,"
the unit doesn't take
up any precious
floor space.**

mirror
images

# light vs. dark

FOR A LONG TIME, IT WAS A DECORATING DICTUM: ALWAYS USE LIGHT, SPACE-expanding colors in a small room. And, naturally, powder rooms fit that category to a T. Although no longer *de rigueur,* pale hues still make sense. Not only do they work magic by visually enlarging the area, they're also quiet by nature, creating the soothing surroundings so often desired in a bathroom.

But for every person who chooses to follow the old school, there's another who's not afraid to break the rules by using dark, dramatic colors. The philosophy here is that, because a powder room already is small, why not make it even more cozy with dark, advancing hues? The resulting intimacy—and excitement—can be hard to duplicate anywhere else.

OPPOSITE: **The tone-on-tone palette in this powder room lends a level of sophistication that befits the room's furnishings.**
LEFT: **Charcoal tiles, a dark mahogany vanity, and a natural granite countertop set the mood in this dark and dramatic bath.**

# making a statement

IF YOU HAD JUST ONE MINUTE TO DESCRIBE yourself to someone, what would you say in those 60 seconds? And so it is with a powder room, where you have a relatively small space in which to make a statement that reflects your personality.

That's why it's important to come up with an attention-getting design. Are you a country enthusiast who's proud of your many collectibles? Be sure to display a few of your favorites in your powder room. Likewise, the absence of such treasures may speak volumes about your decorating preferences; maybe you're a contemporary purist who prefers absolute minimalism. But no matter what your personal preferences may be, let your powder room "have a say" in them!

**OPPOSITE: There's little doubt that the owners of this powder room have a fondness for all things nautical. The maritime mood comes as much from the collectibles as from the shiplap siding and requisite blue paint. RIGHT: Set atop a stone vanity, this hexagonal black Vessel™ from Kohler makes a strong contemporary statement. Gracefully curved handles on the accompanying fittings soften the geometric lines of the basin.**

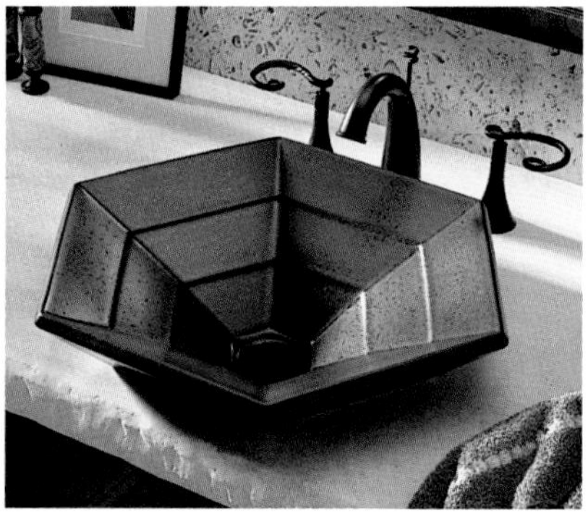

kohler scheme

the case for
space

FOR ALL ITS INHERENTLY INTIMATE CHARM,
the average powder room does bring
with it one drawback. Sometimes it
can be just *too* small—not big enough
to hold all the necessities or even in
which to turn around!

For example, there never seems to
be enough storage space. But with
just a little ingenuity, you can find
room in some of the most unexpect-
ed places. If you have a skirted sink,
stash a basket full of extra towels
beneath it. Or, install a mirrored bath
cabinet and use it to store everything
from towels and washcloths to extra
soap and toilet paper.

But what if you simply want your
powder room to look and live a little
bigger? In that case, the solution
comes in a can: paint. Open a new
door or window by creating your
own *trompe l'oeil* effect. As for the
view, you can look out on a fantasy
world or just your own backyard.

RIGHT: **You can
almost feel the
cool, salt breeze
in this artistically
enhanced bath.
Not only does the**
*trompe l'oeil* **open
up the space, it
opens a whole
new world!**
LEFT: **Looking for
storage space for
bath essentials?
Sometimes, the
only way to go is
up! These mirrored
bath cabinets by
Robern serve the
purpose beautifully.**

details
details

Turning a good bath into a great one comes down to just one thing: attention to detail. As with any other room, it's important to go that last mile and think about how every element will work into the overall plan.

"Details" are more than mere finishing touches. Although accessories are key to a room's success, so is ensuring that each element is right for the space. Does the sink you've picked out convey the mood you want it to? Do the surface materials reflect your chosen style? Only when you're comfortable with the answers to questions like these are you ready to add the appropriate accessories and deem your powder room a success!

OPPOSITE: **Anything but quiet and demure, this bath features pieces that command attention, such as the pedestal lavatory and toilet with French-inspired designs. Carefully chosen appointments leave no question as to the provincial spirit.**
LEFT: **The simple lines of this Vessel™ by Kohler— and the accompanying fittings—echo the soothing mood of the room.**

# the kids' bath

When it comes to planning a child's bathroom, there are some special—even serious—considerations in terms of both safety and space. But there's a lot of room for creativity, too. So once you've thoroughly covered the basics, let your imagination run wild. In short, let yourself be a kid again and have some fun in the decorating process!

CONTRARY TO WHAT MANY PEOPLE believe, children's bathrooms aren't simply otherwise-standard spaces decked out in bright primary or pale pastel colors. Bathrooms earmarked for children need to be carefully designed with their pint-size clients in mind, taking into account their size, abilities, and even their decorating preferences.

Think back to your own childhood. Do you remember stretching up on tiptoe to reach the faucet? It was hard to know if you were turning the water up too high…until you practically burned your fingers. Or, do you recall toilets that left your feet, well, dangling? It wasn't the most comfortable feeling, was it? The solution in both cases is small-scale fixtures, ones that are user-friendly for children and—as they grow—for adults, too.

Depending on the age of the child, abilities also play a part. Are small hands likely to get pinched in hard-to-open drawers? If so, you may want to incorporate easy-to-pull-out wire or wicker baskets. And make sure that children can easily reach towel bars and robe hooks. By putting them within close reach now, you'll be helping your kids develop good habits for the future.

Finally, let young ones get involved in the decorating process. That doesn't mean you have to let them help you pick out every fixture and fitting. But kids develop their favorite colors early on, and by including them, you'll create a place where your child will feel right at home. And don't forget to incorporate a little of his or her personality, too. After all, this room belongs to him or her as much as the master bath belongs to you.

OPPOSITE: **In a child's bathroom, choose hues that your youngsters will not only appreciate while they're young but will also be comfortable with as they grow up.**

measuring up

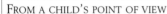

ABOVE: **The countertops in this new bathroom are a full 36 inches high. But to make them more accessible to children, pull-out steps have been built into the cabinets below.**
OPPOSITE: **Decoratively painted cabinetry—plus assorted other mini-prints—makes this bathroom a magical place.**

HERE'S A FACT FOR YOU TO CONSIDER:

For children between 5 and 11 years old, the average eye-level height is 43 inches. So, with countertops ever-rising (36 inches high is the standard), is it any wonder kids have trouble reaching things?

If you have 36-inch-high countertops, find a way to make them work for your children, too. You might provide a six-inch-high step stool; just be sure it's safe and won't tip over easily. Or, if you want to devote this bath exclusively to children, scale the counter down to their size—say, 30 inches high.

FROM A CHILD'S POINT OF VIEW

Many of today's homes have extra-high ceilings, and bathrooms are no exception. But even if your ceilings are standard height, there are some things you can do—visually—to bring them down to child size.

To give the impression of a lower ceiling, stencil a wall border 12 to 18 inches down from the ceiling. To get the same effect, you could paint the ceiling in medium to dark shades, then bring the color down onto the walls for 12 to 18 inches.

By the same token, break up tall expanses of wall by adding a chair rail around the room. To add some real pizzazz, create it with a mix of colorful tiles.

kohler scheme

MORE THAN JUST AN AESTHETIC ELEMENT, COLOR IS AN EMOTIONAL ONE, TOO.
That's why children and adults alike react—both positively and negative-
ly—to certain parts of the spectrum. Case in point: Why do we so often
describe our feelings in such a colorful manner? When we're happy, we're
quick to let others know that we're "in the pink." If we're sad, we're "feeling blue" and if we're jealous, we're "green with envy."

As a result, color becomes more than a passing consideration. Take time
to find out your child's favorite colors and why they're favorites. Maybe

you have an outgoing youngster whose
personality is best reflected by kinetic colors
like red and orange. Or perhaps your shy
youngster is more at home with quiet colors
such as pale blue or green. So, what's *your*
child's color quotient?

OPPOSITE: **Bright,
primary hues are
the rule in this
kids-only bath. The
energizing palette
is a good one for
getting revved up
in the morning.**
LEFT: **More than
merely colorful,
these toilet seats
are safety-minded,
too. Molded hand-
grips on each side
of the scalloped
seats remove any
fear of falling!**

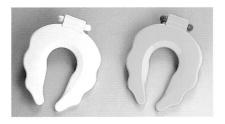

accept the challenge

IMAGINE, IF YOU WILL, LIVING IN A PLAY-
house. It may be a wonderful place,
but it's simply too small to be comfortable. That analogy works for
those with physical disabilities, too.
It's not always easy to live in a world
designed for the able-bodied.

Happily, there are a number of elements you can incorporate to make a
child's bath—or an adult one, for
that matter—more accessible:

■ A bathtub with a hinged door on
the side to provide easy entry

■ Showers fitted with grab bars and
transfer seats

■ For the wheelchair-bound, roll-in
showers, wall-hung sinks, and offset
water controls in the tub

■ Lever handles that can be used by
everyone, including those with
little grip strength.

LEFT: **Although this bathroom was designed
for a child with physical disabilities, it
works equally well for others in the household. The hinged-door bathtub features
integral ledges for balance and safety. And
the wall-hung lavatory, too, is easy to
access with a wheelchair.**

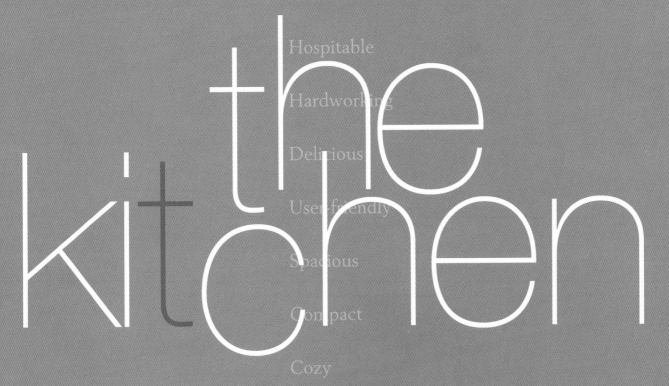

# the kitchen

Warm

Inviting

Aromatic

Hospitable

Hardworking

Delicious

User-friendly

Spacious

Compact

Cozy

Friendly

Efficient

Ready

Innovative

Neighborly

Gourmet

# the eat-in kitchen

There's no longer any doubt: The kitchen is, hands down, the central gathering spot for today's families. As such, it's the main eating area—ready to serve up a quick breakfast, lunch, or even dinner (more likely than not enjoyed in several shifts). Perhaps more than any other room in the house, it reflects how we like to live today—comfortably and casually.

IT'S BEEN QUITE SOME TIME SINCE THE formal dining room was used on a daily basis. That's not to say that it no longer serves a purpose; on the contrary, more people than ever before are opening up their homes to entertain. But in an age where we're most comfortable in well-worn jeans and t-shirts, an equally relaxed dining atmosphere is the norm for day-to-day living.

You may start the morning with an everyone-around-the-table meal. But, if you're like most Americans, there's a very good chance that morning is the only time of the day when that happens. With both parents working and kids involved in all kinds of activities, family members often eat lunch and dinner in shifts, looking only for a comfortable spot in which to take in some nourishment and enjoy a break in the action.

But in spite of these on-the-go lifestyles, one thing needn't be sacrificed—style. There are a million and one ways to incorporate good looks into these eat-in kitchens. Whether you need an area for two or ten, you can tuck a table quietly into a cozy corner, or position it prominently to make it the focal point of the room.

And here's the bonus: By giving your eat-in kitchen some real style, you'll make it more inviting at the same time. Not that your friends and family *need* any more of an invitation. After all, when was the last time you threw a party and people didn't end up in the kitchen? Make yours one of the highlights of your home.

OPPOSITE: **Today's casual lifestyles call for more informal entertaining. This kitchen, for instance, could accommodate two or—set up buffet-style—a crowd.**

# set your own style

THE VERY BEST KITCHEN DESIGNS REFLECT
the owners' personalities, as if they
had whispered something about
themselves to you. But putting personality into a room isn't just about
conveying a sense of yourself to others. It's also about making yourself
feel right at home and surrounding
yourself with your favorite things.

Today's cabinetry, for instance,
can be selected just like a piece of
fine furniture. There's a wealth of
artistry that goes into today's offer-
ings, giving you the solid assurance
that you'll enjoy them for many
years to come.

RIGHT: **The cabinetry
in this sophisticated
kitchen is understat-
ed, yet it's obvious
that there's a great
deal of attention to
detail. It represents
the kind of work
that would have
done the Arts and
Crafts era proud.**
LEFT: **Another view
of the same kitchen
shows the dining
area, illuminated by
natural light during
the day and sus-
pended metal-and-
glass fixtures at
night.**

set your own
style

EVEN THE COLORS IN THIS KITCHEN ARE similar to those used by the Arts and Crafts experts. Muted shades of green, copper, and gold make an appearance in the tile backsplash and, in turn, inspire the room's accent hues.

The jet-black sinks in this space also do their part for the palette. Though they're neutrals that work well with almost anything, here they appear to put the exclamation point on an already successful scheme.

# *that's* entertainment

IT'S ONE THING IF YOU ONLY ENTERTAIN YOUR FAMILY AT THE HOLIDAYS. BUT IT'S quite another if you invite guests over on a regular basis. Then, you need to know how to accommodate them—graciously yet efficiently—so you can enjoy your own party!

If you have the luxury of a spacious kitchen, a good-size island and a separate eating area are party-perfect. Then, you can use the island for a buffet, dish out a sit-down dinner at the table, or use both as serving stations when a couple of couples turns into a crowd. In fact, it's wise to set up several food and beverage stations as it will keep your company mixing and mingling.

Likewise, if you entertain regularly, consider flooring and surfaces that are easy to clean, such as laminate, solid-surface material, and ceramic tile. You'll be glad the morning after!

RIGHT: **Part of the beauty of this kitchen is that its clean, streamlined design allows the guests easy movement throughout the room.**

LEFT: **Devoted solely to storage, the island in this dramatic black-and-yellow kitchen is a great place from which to serve a buffet or simply hang around during a party. For smaller gatherings, a table—teamed with a banquette and chairs—accommodates guests in a more intimate manner.**

another dimension

WHEN IT COMES RIGHT DOWN TO IT, A well-thought-out kitchen is done by the numbers. That is, there are certain formulas to follow:

- Leave 15 to 18 inches of open counter space near the microwave oven for setting hot dishes.
- Leave 18 to 24 inches of counter space on each side of the cooktop. If the cooktop is in the island, leave at least 12 inches on each side.
- Allow 21 inches of standing room between the dishwasher and adjacent counters, other appliances, and cabinets.
- The dishwasher should be placed within 36 inches of the sink for maximum efficiency.

LEFT: **Two wooden stools at the end of the center island comprise a convenient eating area—or simply a place to sit and catch up with the cook.**

TOP RIGHT: **This country kitchen plays the numbers game beautifully. There's plenty of clearance between countertops, and the overhead cabinets aren't so tall that you can't reach the shelves.**

BOTTOM RIGHT: **The warm and welcoming ambience of this nook all but asks you to curl up with a bite of breakfast or an afternoon snack.**

comfort
factors

kohler scheme

IN TERMS OF THE MOOD THEY CONVEY, ALMOST ALL
kitchens are comfortable. But can they be
comfortable in a literal sense, too? The
answer is, unquestionably, yes.

For starters, select dining chairs and bar
stools that have high comfort factors. Don't
purchase them on the basis of beauty only;
instead, take your potential purchase for a
test drive. Sit for a while, even squirm a little, to make sure the seat offers just the
right fit.

By the same token, give careful thought
to the flooring. If you spend hours in the
kitchen, you'll want something comfortable
underfoot. Because they offer resiliency,
laminate and vinyl flooring are two of the
best options.

LEFT: **Before buying
a bar stool, make
sure it's not only
comfortable but
also the right height
for your counter.**
OPPOSITE: **The
comfort of laminate
flooring assures
that you won't be
so "dead on your
feet" that you
won't be able to
enjoy the feast.**

# the cook's kitchen

Whether it's out of necessity—say, space constraints—or a pure choice, many a kitchen is intended for cooking only. But that doesn't mean it needs to be devoid of style. Instead, consider an opportunity to make a statement. So, go ahead. Assemble the necessary ingredients and come up with your own recipe for success!

SOME KITCHENS ARE SINGLE-MINDED. They're devoted to one thing only—cooking. But before you assume they're Lilliputian-size spaces in studio apartments, think again. Although it's true that many kitchens are relegated just to cooking out of necessity, just as many are spacious places that intentionally elect that option. The two-cook kitchen, for example, is becoming more prevalent all the time. Double ovens, multiple sinks, and even twin refrigerators aren't all that surprising to find, either. The luxury of these "extra" appliances makes it easier than ever for two cooks to work side-by-side in the same kitchen.

Space-planning, though, is important in kitchens both large and small. It's essential to put every square inch to work. Maybe you need to incorporate much-needed storage space. Or, perhaps you're trying to fit in a commercial-style range. The point is this: Some of the most creative kitchen plans were designed for minute-size spaces.

So, what—and who—is cooking in your kitchen? Is it the domain of a single chef, or do you share the responsibilities? Whichever is the case, use the best of today's technology to plan your own ultimate cooking quarters.

OPPOSITE: **Because the chef spends so much time in this kitchen, it has a personality flavor that makes it just as inviting as the rest of the house.**
LEFT: **Ceramic tile, like this example from Ann Sacks Tile and Stone, can give instant clues to the owner's tastes. This motif might indicate that the owner likes to fish. Or, it may mean he or she merely likes the dish!**

# knowing your
## needs

DESIGNING A KITCHEN IS A LOT LIKE GETTING
lost out on the highway. Unless you
have a map, you only risk moving far-
ther into the unknown. But there are
things you can do to chart your
course. Specifically, you can make a
list of your needs. Here are a few
things to consider:

■ The work triangle—U-shape,
L-shape, galley, or island

■ Work centers—food storage and
preparation, cooking, baking, cleanup,
planning, recycling, or entertainment

■ Storage—base and overhead cabinets, open shelves, or racks

■ Surfaces—plastic laminate, solid-
surface materials, solid-surface
veneers, natural stone, ceramic tile,
or stainless steel

■ Flooring—laminate, ceramic tile,
vinyl, or hardwood

LEFT: **This cottage-style kitchen incorporates all of the cook's needs—and most of his or her wants, as well.**
OPPOSITE TOP: **At the business end of this kitchen, color is used to define specific cabinets, giving them the appearance of a freestanding piece.**
OPPOSITE BOTTOM: **Kohler's shallow-tray sink is perfect for small jobs such as washing a few dishes or rinsing vegetables.**

k o h l e r   s c h e m e

in duplicate

kohler scheme

IT'S NOT THAT KITCHENS WITH TWO SEPARATE work areas are new. It's just that they keep growing in popularity.

Typically, in a two-cook kitchen, each work area has its own sink—the most frequent stop during meal preparation and cleanup. In addition to the sink, the main work area is defined by the refrigerator and stove or cooktop. Plus, the second zone may include specialty appliances.

To work out the logistics—and make sure one cook doesn't get in the other's way—you need at least a 48-inch walkway between counters so users can comfortably share the space. Two-cook kitchens need not be grand, but they should be at least 13 feet wide and 16 feet long.

OPPOSITE: **Islands designed for distinctly different purposes take center stage in this gourmet kitchen. The twin refrigerators let you know that cooking is serious business here.**
LEFT: **More and more kitchens are being outfitted with two sinks—if not three. Here, the small sink handles food preparation and the large one shortcuts cleanup.**

# on the surface

YOUR COUNTERTOPS GO THROUGH A LOT; THEY'RE CONSTANTLY EXPOSED TO MOISture, heat, and germs. So you'll want to choose surface materials that will stand up to the task and still look great when guests arrive.

*Decorative laminate* is inexpensive, low-maintenance, and comes in a variety of patterns and colors. It resists grease and stains but won't stand up to sharp knives or hot pans. *Ceramic tile,* too, comes in a wide assortment of colors and patterns, and it has durability on its side. Tile handles hot pans without scorching and is stain- and moisture-resistant, as well.

Durability is a selling point for *solid-surface materials,* too. Because they're nonporous, they resist mildew and stains. They can also be refinished to keep them looking new. If your budget isn't ready for the solid-surface materials, though, think about *solid-surface veneers,* thin sheets that offer substantial savings over solid materials.

RIGHT: **Ceramic tile comes in a variety of sizes, from one-inch mosaics to 8x10-inch rectangles. You can customize your countertop by using a combination of solid-color and patterned tiles.**
LEFT: **Although they're available at a lower price than standard solid-surface materials, solid-surface veneers—like these from Wilsonart—can accommodate contrasting-color edge treatments for special effects.**

# sink it!

ALMOST EVERY KITCHEN ACTIVITY REVOLVES AROUND THE SINK. SO, IT'S IMPORTANT to pick one that's both versatile and durable.

*Enameled cast iron* is one of the most popular choices for sinks, first and foremost because the material is durable. Its advantages don't end there, though. Enameled cast iron resists chipping and will keep its shine even after years of use. And, unlike stainless-steel sinks that tend to blend into the background, enameled cast-iron options—in their myriad colors—command attention.

Because it's durable, lightweight, and—perhaps best of all—inexpensive, *stainless steel* also has a considerable following. Before you purchase a stainless steel sink, however, consider the quality of the metal itself; a heavier steel will better resist denting.

If neither cast iron nor stainless steel suit your particular needs, there are other options. Vitreous china, quartz composite, and solid surfacing are just a few of the materials you may want to consider.

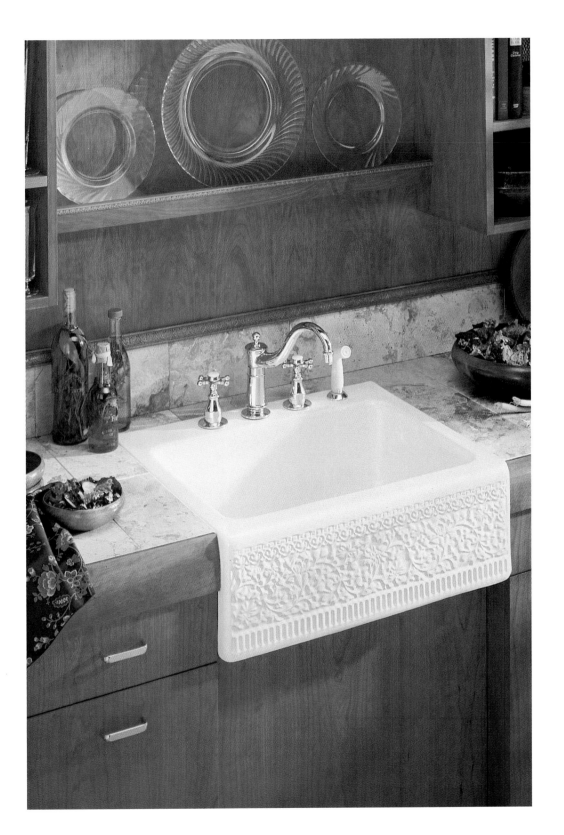

LEFT: **With a delicately carved apron and vintage-style fittings, this sink is filled with nostalgic charm.**
OPPOSITE LEFT: **Teamed with a creamy white solid-surface countertop, this cast-iron sink from Kohler makes a stunning color statement.**
OPPOSITE RIGHT: **Many of today's stainless-steel sinks—like this one from Kohler—come with cutting board, colander, and rinse-basket options.**

## hot hues

HOT COLORS ALWAYS FIND THEIR WAY TO THE
kitchen. So what's the latest news in
hues? In short, the hottest shades are,
well, cool. Subdued blues and greens
are among those on the most-wanted
list today, thanks in large part to their
soothing qualities.

All of these shades can be traced
back to Mother Nature herself.
Turquoise, cobalt blue, forest green—
they're all part of nature's palette.
So, it's no surprise that shades
inspired by stone and minerals are
also becoming predominant.

And how do these hues fit into the
kitchen? They show up in everything
from fixtures to furnishings. Don't be
afraid to show *your* true colors!

OPPOSITE: **Red-hot
cabinetry raises the
temperature in
this kitchen. Deep
green accents,
though—in the wall-
hung cabinet, tiled
sink surround, and
counter edging—
keep the scheme
from boiling over.**
RIGHT: **With its
brilliant cobalt
color, the Cilantro™
self-rimming sink by
Kohler can serve
as a focal point in
its own right.**

put it in
neutral

kohler scheme

EVEN THOSE WITH COLOR CONFIDENCE sometimes hesitate when it comes to planning a kitchen. The major elements—large appliances, cabinetry, and flooring—represent sizable investments. And, as such, they aren't the kinds of things most people will be eager to replace every time color trends change.

But you still can keep current with color and stick to your budget, too. Just go with a neutral scheme— anything from stark white to dramatic black—and add color with your favorite accents. You'll not only save money, but you'll be able to change the look of your kitchen on a regular basis, too.

LEFT: **The dark granite countertops are in stark contrast to the light cabinetry in this kitchen. So where does the color come in? With plants and treasured accessories arranged throughout the room.** OPPOSITE: **Warm wood tones take a neutral stance in this kitchen, made more dramatic by black and stainless steel accents. Lest it become too dark, though, there's plenty of natural light.**

# universal charm

IT'S LONG BEEN APPRECIATED BY PEOPLE WITH PHYSICAL DISABILITIES, BUT UNIVERSAL design now is getting more recognition by the masses. It's not unlikely, for example, that you could be in an accident or that an elderly parent may come to live with you. Here are a few things you can to do comply with universal-design guidelines:

- Lower light switches or install voice-activated light switches.
- Use touch-latch doors—no knobs or pulls.
- Build a step stool into the toe kick of base cabinets for help in reaching wall cabinets.
- Store dishes in a 42-inch-high wall cabinet set on the floor, making access convenient.
- Elevate the dishwasher 6 to 16 inches to minimize stooping.
- Leave the area under the cooktop and sink open so a wheelchair can fit underneath.

RIGHT: **Beneath this 30-inch-high cooktop, retractable doors can accommodate a wheelchair. And for anyone who suffers from a height disadvantage, a two-step stool is ready to give a leg up.**
LEFT: **The undercounter opening isn't this sink's only nod to universal design. Kohler designed an easy-grasp lever handle for the faucet that makes the fixture more accessible, too.**

THE PANTRY IS AN IDEA WHOSE TIME HAS COME—AGAIN. FROM HIS BUFFER ZONE separating the kitchen and the dining room, the butler once transformed the flurry of food preparation into a smooth meal presentation. Today, we're more or less on our own—and that's not the only thing that's changed. In contemporary pantries, warming ovens, small refrigerators, and microwave ovens now take the hassle out of serving a crowd. And, for easy cleanup, there are second sinks, garbage disposals, trash compactors, and dishwashers. Even wine racks and drawers for fine linens rank high on today's list of desired pantry amenities.

In short, the pantry works hard to keep things organized and running smoothly. Even a butler couldn't do it better.

RIGHT: **Tucked behind the bar, this modest-size pantry holds gourmet foods, serving pieces, and a collection of wine. And, because it also performs so beautifully, the door often is left wide open.**

LEFT: **In this era of casual entertaining, guests often continue to converse with their host as he or she works in the pantry. So it's no surprise to see these spaces decorated just like any other room in the house.**

## *Gracious Living* Order Form

To order *Gracious Living* in magazine format or hard-cover book edition,
fill in the appropriate blanks below:

*Gracious Living* **magazine** $5 each x _____ *(no. of copies)* + $1.95 *(shipping)* = $_____
*Gracious Living* **book** $15 each* x _____ *(no. of copies)* + $1.95 *(shipping)* = $_____

Total Amount $_____

*Available September 1, 1997.

NAME

ADDRESS

CITY                          STATE                          ZIP

TELEPHONE                     CREDIT CARD NUMBER             EXPIRATION DATE

SIGNATURE                     ❑ MASTERCARD   ❑ VISA

Make check payable to: Kohler Coordinates, 444 Highland Drive, Kohler, WI 53044-9902
or call **1-800-772-1814 Ext. 209.**

---

## *Gracious Living* Order Form

To order *Gracious Living* in magazine format or hard-cover book edition,
fill in the appropriate blanks below:

*Gracious Living* **magazine** $5 each x _____ *(no. of copies)* + $1.95 *(shipping)* = $_____
*Gracious Living* **book** $15 each* x _____ *(no. of copies)* + $1.95 *(shipping)* = $_____

Total Amount $_____

*Available September 1, 1997.

NAME

ADDRESS

CITY                          STATE                          ZIP

TELEPHONE                     CREDIT CARD NUMBER             EXPIRATION DATE

SIGNATURE                     ❑ MASTERCARD   ❑ VISA

Make check payable to: Kohler Coordinates, 444 Highland Drive, Kohler, WI 53044-9902
or call **1-800-772-1814 Ext. 209.**

---

## *Gracious Living* Order Form

To order *Gracious Living* in magazine format or hard-cover book edition,
fill in the appropriate blanks below:

*Gracious Living* **magazine** $5 each x _____ *(no. of copies)* + $1.95 *(shipping)* = $_____
*Gracious Living* **book** $15 each* x _____ *(no. of copies)* + $1.95 *(shipping)* = $_____

Total Amount $_____

*Available September 1, 1997.

NAME

ADDRESS

CITY                          STATE                          ZIP

TELEPHONE                     CREDIT CARD NUMBER             EXPIRATION DATE

SIGNATURE                     ❑ MASTERCARD   ❑ VISA

Make check payable to: Kohler Coordinates, 444 Highland Drive, Kohler, WI 53044-9902
or call **1-800-772-1814 Ext. 209.**

# BUSINESS REPLY MAIL

First Class Mail Permit No. 1 Kohler, WI

Postage will be paid by addressee

Kohler Coordinates
Kohler Co.
Advertising Department
444 Highland Drive
Kohler WI 53044-9902

llıluıllıllıuıluıluıluıllluluıluılluuuluıluıll

# BUSINESS REPLY MAIL

First Class Mail Permit No. 1 Kohler, WI

Postage will be paid by addressee

Kohler Coordinates
Kohler Co.
Advertising Department
444 Highland Drive
Kohler WI 53044-9902

llıluıllıllıuıluıluıluıllluluıluılluuuluıluıll

# BUSINESS REPLY MAIL

First Class Mail Permit No. 1 Kohler, WI

Postage will be paid by addressee

Kohler Coordinates
Kohler Co.
Advertising Department
444 Highland Drive
Kohler WI 53044-9902

llıluıllıllıuıluıluıluıllluluıluılluuuluıluıll

the well-stocked pantry

# getting back to basics

Personal preferences play a large part in the selection of kitchen and bath products. But don't be tempted to shove practicality offstage! Materials, amenities, and—perhaps most important—pricing should all be taken into consideration, too. On these eight pages you'll find the basic information you'll need to make well-informed choices.

What should you think about when planning a bath? For starters, plumbing products; the sheer variety on the market today is mind-boggling.

## PLUMBING PRODUCTS

There's a bevy of beautiful fixtures on the market today. Here's some help in sorting them out:

### Lavatories

Lavatories come in four basic types: pedestal, wall-mount, above-counter, and countertop.

Pedestal lavatories feature a basin that's positioned at a comfortable standing height. Offered in a wealth of decorative options, pedestal sinks can bring instant drama to a bathroom.

Wall-mount lavatories have a basin hung from the wall at a desired height. Is there someone particularly tall in the family? If so, you might want to raise the sink an inch or two. Likewise, if you're designing a child's bath, bring the sink down to his or her level.

Countertop and above-counter lavatories are designed for used with vanities and countertops. Countertop lavs have several options, too; they can install as self-rimming, tile-in, undercounter-mount, or vanity-top.

Lavatory material choices include the following:

- *Cast iron* is so durable that it will seemingly last forever, putting it in a class by itself for life-time performance. Plus, it comes in a wide variety of high-gloss colors which can not only create an eye-catching focal point but also retain their shine through years and years of wear.
- *Vitreous china* or *fireclay* are used to make a great number of lavatories that can be formed into many a stunning shape.
- *Glass* is most often found in contemporary baths, where glass basins are likely to be set atop a counter.
- *Stainless steel* is making its way into the bathroom; look for heavy steel (about 18-gauge or 20-gauge) in satin or mirror finishes.
- *Solid-surface materials* are stain-resistant and easy to repair. In addition, they can be molded to create a continuous sink and countertop. Keep in mind, however, that they are more expensive.

### Faucets and Fittings

Basically, there are two types of faucets: a standard spout or an arch (a gooseneck or crescent, for instance). As for fittings, handles are offered in a variety of styles, including cross handles, levers, wrist-blades, or cylinders.

Standard faucets usually cost between $50 and $150. Center-set faucets are typically less expensive than wide-spread models of this price point.

From there, mid-range faucets run about $150 to $500 and luxury faucets typically over $500.

### Bathtubs

In terms of bathtubs, there's an endless array of sizes, shapes, and colors. Your choice will depend, to a large degree, on available space and what amenities are important to you.

- *Clawfoot tub*—this traditional style is adapted from Victorian times.

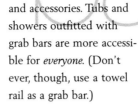

- *Rectangular tub*—a popular style, it can be used alone or combined with a shower.
- *Round or oval tub*—this is a show-stopper and provides a deep soak.
- *Corner tub*—a real space-saver, this style is perfectly suited to take advantage of a corner window view.
- *Barrier-free tub*—with a hinged door, accessibility is easier than in a standard model.

Finally, be sure to consider materials. The most durable material is undoubtedly cast iron because the enameled finish resists staining and scratching. Plus, cast iron helps maintain water temperature and minimize the noise of running water.

As for acrylic and fiberglass, they resist flexing, chipping, and cracking and are—at the same time—easy to maintain. Another economical alternative to acrylic is Vikrell.

**Tub Faucets and Fittings**
When it's time to "fill 'er up," what's your preference for faucets and fittings?

The most familiar are standard wall-mount faucets. They're not, however, created equal. Some feature Rite-Temp Pressure Balanced Mixers™ that keep temperatures constant (within three degrees) to protect you from scalding or freezing.

In terms of deck and rim-mount tub fillers, be sure to look for washerless ceramic valving. It will control the flow of water under any conditions and is easy to maintain, too. Likewise, look for pull-out sprays with deck or wall-mount faucets that will give you more flexability.

When outfitting your tub, don't forget grab bars and accessories. Tubs and showers outfitted with grab bars are more accessible for *everyone*. (Don't ever, though, use a towel rail as a grab bar.)

**Whirlpools**
Once you've experienced a whirlpool, you'll see why so many people are opting for them. Not only do they offer up to ten jets, but many include integral heaters, too. Consider water capacity, though, especially if water conservation is a priority; whirlpools can hold anywhere from 50 to 150 gallons of water.

The most economical whirlpools start at $700 to $1,000 while luxury models can top out at $5,000.

**Showers**
Today's showers are every bit as luxurious as bathtubs and whirlpools. Body sprays, multiple showerheads, and therapeutic steam are just a few of the options. Beyond the shower itself, you'll need to find the right faucetry. You can spend anywhere from $50 to $1,000 getting the right spray—be it a fixed showerhead or a body spray with jets mounted on the wall.

**Given their fill of plumbing products, bathrooms can sometimes be a design challenge. And so, for that matter, are kitchens. If you're looking for professional assistance for either, consider calling on the talents of a certified bath designer (CBD) or certified kitchen designer (CKD). For a listing of certified kitchen and bath designers in your area, contact the National Kitchen and Bath Association, 687 Willow Grove St., Hackettstown, NJ 07840.**

## Toilets

Toilets have recently stepped up in style, especially when coordinated in a suite with a lavatory and tub. They're available as standard two-piece models (with a tank and bowl) as well as streamlined, one-piece units.

- *Two-piece.* This, the most traditional design, comes in a wide variety of styles. The new low-flush toilets are characterized by taller tanks and steeper bowls.
- *One-piece.* These toilets are seamless, space-saving designs and are perfect for today's contemporary home. They are easy to clean and usually include both the seat and cover.

In your search for bathroom toilets, keep in mind that all new models are required to use no more than 1.6 gallons per flush, compared to 3.5 and 5 gallons in the past. This can this save as much as 20,000 gallons a year in the average home, which translates to a considerable saving on your water bill!

The European-inspired bidet, too, is growing in popularity throughout the United States. Because it functions as a sit-down wash basin, a bidet is installed along the same wall as the toilet, and is typically chosen to match the toilet's design.

## CABINETS

Simply put, the same kind of cabinetry used in the kitchen has long been used in the bathroom, too. And, although that particular kind of storage—more often than not, base cabinets—is still used to a large degree, there are plenty of other storage options, too.

For starters, don't neglect wall-hung cabinets. They're the ideal solution if you're short on floor space and have nowhere to go but up. Again, standard cabinetry like that found in your kitchen makes for up-and-out-of-the-way

storage space. But don't forget space-expanding mirrored bath cabinets, either. No longer a tiny wooden box with a mirror, the modern bath cabinet can match other bath fixtures and accessories in terms of design, function, and practicality. It can be purchased in modular systems to suit your specific needs, with any mirror and trim type you like. And don't think you need to limit its use to medicine. Although the standard depth for most mirrored bath cabinets is four inches or less, new models in six- and eight-inch depths are becoming more common—making room for toilet paper, lotions and creams, even small towels.

Furniture, too, is making its way into the bathroom. You might, for instance, consider a freestanding storage piece. Be sure, however, that it can stand up to the inevitable moisture of a bathroom.

## COUNTERTOPS

Because they work just as hard in the bathroom as they do in the kitchen, countertops require materials that are equally durable. Thus, the same kinds of materials are appropriate—solid-surface materials, solid-surface veneers, decorative laminates, natural stone, and ceramic tile (see *pages 24-25*). Don't automatically assume, though, that you should use the same materials in the kitchen and bath. Consider, first, how differently the two spaces function and make the best decision for each.

## TILE IN THE BATH

With its myriad uses, tile is a true bathing beauty. Tile works on walls, floors, shower and tub surrounds, even vanity counters and backsplashes.

*Tile walls* are appropriate for almost any bathroom, but think beyond the standard 4x4-inch tiles. Consider six- or eight-inch squares or rectangular tiles set in any number of patterns. You might, for instance, choose a pastel palette and apply the tile in a patchwork pattern. Or, create a chair rail with smaller accent tiles.

*Tile floors* in the bathroom need special consideration. Because you're often barefoot in the bathroom, slip-resistance is a crucial factor. Look for matte finish or textured tiles. Small tiles, too—with their many grout lines—can provide good traction.

Tile is a good choice, too, for *showers and tub surrounds.* Glazed ceramic tile, for instance, has the advantage of being natural-ly water-resistant so, when installed on the proper substrate, it provides a sur-face that will last for years. And, it's especially impor-tant that shower floors have slip-proof tiles for safety purposes. All this concern for safety doesn't mean you need to give up glamour, though. You can give shower or tub walls dramatic impact with a

decorative approach to tile—with a traditional frieze, intricate moldings, or even high-relief tiles. Or, create a shower that contrasts the rest of the room by giving it a self-contained design.

Don't overlook the fact, either, that tile makes a hard-wearing *countertop* that will withstand the water-soaked nature of the sink area. It's imperative, however, that you wipe up

water so it doesn't sit on the tile and wear away at the grout. (Because it's more water-resistant, use a vinyl-based grout or one with latex or acrylic addi-tives.) Keep in mind that your countertop tile can run up the wall and serve as a backsplash, too.

## LIGHTING

Bathrooms need appropri-ate light for tasks such as grooming, but that light should also be complimen-tary. Incandescent lighting, with red and yellow over-tones, is without a doubt the most flattering.

Keep in mind, too, that it's best to take a balanced approach by using multi-ple fixtures in strategic locations. You'll need lighting, for instance, over the shower/tub area (making sure the lighting is rated for damp loca-tions), above the toilet, and—of course—near the vanity. Beyond providing the proper balance, light directed from a variety of sources will result in fewer harsh shadows.

Specifically, for groom-ing purposes, cross-illumination is essential. That is, it's important to have equal light on both sides of your face. Sconces are an excellent way to achieve that as are strip or side lights. Incandescent

bulbs create a softer, more flattering light. Don't for-get, either, that dimmers will allow you to simulate a wide variety of lighting conditions.

Pre-lit mirrored bath cabinets have an advantage in that the interior lighting will help you find what-ever you may need in the middle of the night. For the most part, they are contemporary in style, although you can find a few Victorian models.

If, on the other hand, you have a mirrored wall over your vanity, you may opt to add sconces right onto the mirrored surface. Simply place one on the right and one on the left and position both just slightly above your head. For this kind of installa-tion, though, you'll want to consult an electrician.

## WALL TREATMENTS

The wall treatments in your bathroom need to be more than aesthetically pleasing, they also have to keep practical matters in check. For tub and shower surrounds, for instance, pick a waterproof material such as ceramic tile, stone, or solid surfacing.

Paint or wall coverings work well in areas that won't be splashed with a great deal of water. (And, you can get a lot of cre-

ative mileage with decora-tive paint finishes.) But be sure to stick with easy-to-clean options; paint with a high sheen or vinyl-coated wall coverings are two particularly good choices. It's important to use moisture-resistant adhesives designed for vinyl wall cov-erings rather than ordinary wallpaper paste. And remember, too, that even with waterproof surfaces, adequate ventila-tion is an absolute must.

## VENTILATION

Moisture is inherent to the bathroom, but you can make sure it doesn't linger any longer than necessary by investing in a good ven-tilation system. A fan, too, will remove odors from your bathroom in an effi-cient manner.

Though ventilation is by no means an aesthetic addition, it's worth the money to install a quality duct system. You can spend as little as $20 for a simple duct. But a good mid-range model will cost about $150 and, at the high end of the spectrum, you can get a fan for approximately $200 that will go so far as to include sensors that detect changes in the humidity level.

getting back to basics

BEFORE YOU SET OUT TO design the kitchen of your dreams, you should know that there's more to it than choosing a new sink.

### WHAT'S YOUR STYLE?

Because it will affect the kind of furnishings and appliances you will choose, you'll need to start by defining your style.

**Determine Your Kitchen Use**

First and foremost, how will your kitchen be used? Is it a small space in which family members stop only long enough to put something in the microwave? Or is it a place where everybody sits down together for a meal and enjoys each other's company? Is it a family-only area, or do you entertain there on a regular basis? Does it need to incorporate areas other than cooking and eating? Home office and entertainment areas, for instance, are showing up in more and more kitchens today.

**Elements of Style**

It's equally important for you to consider your decorating preferences. Are you a loyal traditionalist? Or is sleek contemporary design more your style? Whatever the answer, you're sure to find elements that will reflect those tastes.

### FLOOR PLANS

Researchers in the 1950s determined that positioning the sink, refrigerator, and range on the points of an imaginary triangle made the kitchen work more efficiently. With this layout, cooks take fewer steps during the preparation and cleanup of a meal.

For utmost efficiency, the total distance between the sink, refrigerator, and range should be between 12 and 26 feet. As you plan your strategy, consider these possibilities:

**The Galley Kitchen**

Two parallel work counters form the compact galley kitchen. Because this layout requires little space, it's a favorite in places with diminutive dimensions. In the galley kitchen, the refrigerator and sink typically occupy one stretch of cabinetry while the range is on the opposite wall. Keep in mind that there should be a minimum of four feet between countertops.

**The U-Shaped Kitchen**

As its name implies, three lengths of cabinetry form a U, with one appliance in each length. This configuration isn't efficient, however, when cabinetry follows the walls in a large kitchen, creating a triangle that exceeds 26 feet. In that case, a better solution may be to compress the work triangle with a peninsula that forms one leg of the U.

**The L-Shaped Kitchen**

In the L-shape plan, two appliances are set in one stretch of cabinets while the remaining one occupies the second perpendicular stretch. This layout works well unless the two appliances on the single wall lack sufficient counter space between them. Without enough work room, you'll take extra steps to get to a countertop you can use. Plan at least 36 inches of counter space between appliances.

**The Island Kitchen**

Float a freestanding length of cabinetry near the center of an L-shape kitchen and you have an island floor plan. Positioned correctly and equipped with a cooktop or sink, the island becomes one point of the work triangle and helps route traffic out of the cook's way. Put the appliances on opposite walls in your kitchen, however, and your island becomes a stumbling block. In order for traffic to pass between the cook and the island, create aisles at least four feet wide. Be sure there is ample clearance, too, between the oven or dishwasher door and another workstation.

Finally, keep in mind that with the latest refrigeration options—going beyond convention to include convenient under-counter and in-drawer styles—it's easier than ever to compact the kitchen work triangle and put essential appliances precisely where you need them most.

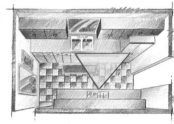

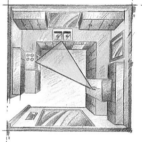

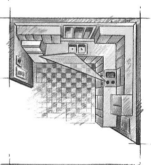

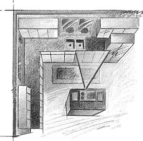

## CABINETRY

The choices in cabinetry—frame or frameless—are easy to spot. Frameless cabinetry features a continuous surface of doors and drawer fronts. On frame cabinets, the reveal (exposed edges) shows around doors and drawers.

The biggest advantage of framed cabinets is their stability. With the frame providing support, the back, bottom, top, and sides of a cabinet can be constructed from thinner material. A disadvantage, though, is that door and drawer openings are smaller on framed cabinets than on frameless units. As a result, drawers and roll-out accessories will be smaller than the overall width of the cabinet.

The advantage of frameless cabinets is accessibility. With no frame to steal space, the cabinets open up to their full capacity. What's the disadvantage? Planning a layout with frameless units requires expertise; it's important to allow door clearances that may not be needed with framed units.

In addition to frame choices, you need to understand how cabinets are manufactured. There are three general categories: stock, semicustom, and custom.

Time, money, and space can be the determining factors. With your plan and a list of your storage needs in hand, shop around; styles and prices will vary from dealer to dealer.

### Stock Cabinets
Stock cabinetry is the least expensive choice, but also has the fewest options. That's because manufacturing necessitates standardization of sizes.

### Semicustom Cabinets
Semicustom cabinets are built by a manufacturer to fit your kitchen. You specify sizes and interior fittings. Some semicustom cabinets don't vary much in size from preassembled stock cabinets. Still, you're likely to have a bigger selection.

### Custom Cabinets
Custom cabinetry offers the advantage of special sizes, unusual designs, custom finishes, and interior fittings. For example, you can specify extra height for base cabinets if you're tall, and extra depth if you need more countertop or storage space. Built on-site, custom cabinets are the most expensive and require the most time from ordering to installation.

## COUNTERTOPS

In terms of countertops, choose a material that will stand up to whatever your family dishes out.

### Solid-Surface Materials
Durability is perhaps the greatest selling point of solid-surface material, a stonelike synthetic sub-

stance. Solid-surface material measures one-half inch thick, and color runs through out so nicks are seldom noticeable.

Because it's nonporous, too, solid-surface material resists mildew and stains. If the countertop is scorched or scratched, minor damage can be repaired with sandpaper.

The cost for solid-surface material starts at about $100 per running foot, installed.

### Solid-Surface Veneer
This is a great way to enjoy the advantages of solid-surface material without the cost. A solid-surface veneer consists of a thin $\frac{1}{8}$-inch-thick sheet of solid-surface material that's adhered to a parti-

cleboard substrate, much like a laminate.

The veneer is seamless and nonporous to resist stains. Nicks and burns can be buffed out with a plastic scrub pad. And, like their solid-surface counterparts, they come in a vast assortment of colors and designs.

Solid-surface veneer can offer a 30 percent savings over conventional solid-surface material. Costs typically run from $70 per running foot, installed.

### Decorative Laminate
Decorative laminate is probably the most popular countertop material, and it's easy to see why. It's inexpensive as well as low-maintenance, and comes in a variety of colors, patterns, and textures.

Decorative laminate is simply a $\frac{1}{16}$-inch-thick surfacing bonded to $\frac{3}{4}$-inch plywood or particleboard,

but the look it provides can be anything but simple. Consider giving a decorative laminate countertop a rolled edge, or trim the edges with beveled wood or metal inlays to create your own custom look.

Scratches and chips are harder to see on most solid-color laminates, where color runs through the entire sheet. Solid-color products also can be routed to create decorative effects. Laminate prices start at about $25 per running foot, installed.

### Ceramic Tile

Tile is durable and available in many colors, patterns, and sizes, from 1-inch squares to 8x10-inch rectangles. Customize your countertop—and cut costs—by using a combination of solid-color and patterned tiles.

Tile handles hot pans without scorching and is moisture-resistant. And, generally, a quick wipe with a damp cloth is all it takes to clean tile. Grout joints are susceptible to stains, but in most cases, they can be removed with scouring powder and household bleach.

The price of solid-color tiles starts at about $5 per square foot, installed. Patterned tiles start at about $2 apiece.

### Natural Stone

Granite and marble offer beauty and durability for countertops. But it's their expense that puts them out of consideration for some homeowners.

The cost of stone starts at about $120 per running foot. Installation also is costly, since stone is heavy and hard to cut. Regular waxing and polishing is necessary to maintain the stone's luster.

Granite is the most popular stone for countertops. It cleans easily and can handle water, hot pots, and sharp knives. It also resists most stains and can be sealed to protect against all stains. Marble is more porous than granite and is more susceptible to staining.

## FLOORING

Almost anything is possible on your floor—from laminate wood look-alikes to rich tile. And although flooring can make a stylish statement, make sure your choice will still handle the everyday wear and tear of heavy traffic—and the inevitable spills.

### Tile

Easy maintenance and durability are the main assets of ceramic-tile flooring. Tile also presents unlimited decorating possibilities. The surface, however, is harder on feet—and dropped dishes—than either vinyl or wood.

Ceramic tiles come in collections of mix-and-match colors and shapes. You'll find anything from 1x1- to 16x16-inch squares and geometric shapes in assorted sizes.

Glazed tile is a good choice in the kitchen because liquids can't soak in. But they may show wear in high-traffic areas. Likewise, unglazed tile can also work in the kitchen, but will require more care.

The installed price of ceramic tile starts at about $10 per square foot. The price rises, though, if the subfloor needs work to accommodate installation.

### Wood

Wood flooring complements any residence and it blends beautifully with most color schemes. New moisture-resistant finishes are increasing wood's popularity in the kitchen. Wood also is a forgiving surface for those cooks who spend a lot of time on their feet. Prices generally start at about $7 per square foot, installed.

### Laminate

If you like the look of wood but want a floor that can better withstand a beating, consider laminate flooring. Some laminates install in planks like wood, while others are available in tiles that replicate stone and other finishes. Laminate typically sells for about $8 per square foot, installed.

### Vinyl

Vinyl flooring is a natural for families with children. A dropped glass has a good chance of surviving, and spills clean up easily. The softness of the flooring also cuts down on noise.

Vinyl, which starts at about $4 per square foot, is available in sheets and tiles. Sheet vinyl is more expensive than a comparative grade of vinyl tile, but avoids the many seams that tiles show.

## SINKS AND FAUCETS

Nearly every kitchen activity revolves around the sink. In many cases, you fill pots, wash vegetables, scrub dishes, and clean hands all in one spot. If

getting back to basics

you only have room for one sink, make sure it's one that's versatile. If, on the other hand, you have the luxury of space, consider multiple sinks; a small one in the food prep area is a good choice.

### Sink Shapes

Some of the standard sink options include single, double, triple, corner, and round sinks. Or, you may want to choose modular units and create your own setup.

Basically, kitchen sinks are made of two materials: cast iron or stainless steel.

- *Cast iron,* by far the most popular, is so durable that it will seemingly last forever, plus it comes in a wide variety of high-gloss colors which retain their shine through years and years of wear.
- *Stainless steel* is gradually making its way into the kitchen; look for heavy steel (about 18-gauge or 20-gauge) in satin or mirror finishes.

### Sink Mounts

A sink's mounting, as much as its configuration, will affect its look—as well as its efficiency.

- *Top-mount or self-rimming sinks* fit over the countertop and are easy to install. The built-up sides of the sink help keep water from splashing onto the countertop.
- *Flush-mount sinks* are those that line up level with the countertop. Most often used in tiled-in installations, they're not as adept at catching splashes but do provide a smooth look.
- *Undermount sinks* are recessed below the countertop and work well with solid-surfaces.

### Spouting Off

Kitchen faucets don't just deliver water; they can conserve water and control its temperature, too. Faucet spouts range from standard to gooseneck to those with a pull-out spray head.

### APPLIANCES

Kitchen appliances can make or break your kitchen design. With that in mind, consider what you're looking for.

### Refrigerators

There are three types of standard refrigerators— top-mount, bottom-mount, and side-by-side— plus a new style that fits into cabinetry.

When searching for the right refrigerator, balance the cost of any "extras" against how often you'll use them, and don't forget less flashy considerations such as quality construction, quiet operation, and automatic defrost.

### Oven/Range Options

The way ovens are used in most kitchens today is a reflection of families' busy lifestyles.

- A conventional oven is the type most people are familiar with. You can expect prices for conventional wall ovens to start at about $400.
- Convection ovens circulate heated air for faster, more even cooking. And many ovens offer both conventional and convection operation. Prices for combination wall ovens begin at about $1,500.
- The everyday convenience of the microwave oven has made it nearly indispensable in today's kitchen. A midsize unit sells for about $200.
- A range, with the cooktop and the oven in one unit, starts at about $500; slide-in units are about $900.

# sources and resources

**Kohler Co.**
444 Highland Dr.
Kohler, WI 53044
414-457-4441
www.kohlerco.com

**Ann Sacks**
8120 NE 33rd Dr.
Portland, OR 97211
503-281-7751
www.annsackstile.com

**Canac**
360 John St.
Thornhill, Ontario
Canada
L3T 3M9
905-881-2153

**Dacor**
950 S. Raymond Ave.
Pasadena, CA 91109
818-799-1000
www.dacorappl.com

**Daltile**
7834 Hawn Frwy.
Dallas, TX 75217
1-800-933-TILE
www.daltile.com

**Dutch Boy Paint**
101 Prospect Ave.
Cleveland, OH 44115
1-800-828-5669

**Robern**
7 Wood Ave.
Bristol, PA 19007
215-826-9800
www.robern.com

**Sub-Zero**
4717 Hammersley Rd.
Madison, WI 53711
1-800-444-7820
marketing@sub-zero
freezer.com

**Wilsonart International**
2400 Wilson Place
Temple, TX 76503
1-800-433-3222
www.wilsonart.com

**Cover** *Designer: Mary Reid, Kohler Co., Kohler, WI 53044.* Vessel Turnings in Stoneware, IV Georges faucets and accessories, Steeping Bath whirlpool in Biscuit—Kohler Co. 4x4 Ross Verona Pavimenti tile—Ann Sacks Tile. Mission Door cabinets in Natural Maple—Canac. Paint "Cocoa Seeds" 4-Y-1—Dutch Boy Paint.

**Inside Front Cover** Laminate room divider in Natural Almond—Wilsonart International. **Page 2, Top:** *Designer: William M. Manly, FASID, 301 N. Water St., Suite 700, Milwaukee, WI 53202 (414) 291-5200.*

Birthday Bath in Almond, IV Georges Console Table, Antique Faucets—Kohler Co. **Bottom left:** Series M Cabinets, mirror, MPHL halogen wall sconces, MTS sink modules—Robern (photograph courtesy of Better Homes & Gardens®

Special Interest Publications). **Bottom right:** Tacoma Limed cabinetry—Canac.

**Page 3, top left:** Down to Earth Glass tiles—Ann Sacks. **Top right:** *Designer: O. Franco Nonahal Kitchen Studio, 355 S. Old Woodward Ave., Brimingham, MI 48009; 810-645-0410.* Model 550 SS—Sub-Zero. **Middle right:** Laminate postformed countertop in Granite—Wilsonart International. **Bottom left:** Diamonds floor tile, 8x8 Rainer with Navy accent dots—Daltile. **Bottom right:** Epicure 48-inch cooktop #ESG486—Dacor.

**Page 4** Vessels Turnings, Life in the Country undercounter kitchen sinks with Revival faucet—Kohler Co.

**Page 6** Vessels Iron Bell lavatory in Cobalt Blue with wall-mount bracket—Kohler Co. 4-inch Hex Fiel Tile, 2x2

Topiary Inserts from the Topiary series—Ann Sacks. Mission Maple Natural Cellia cabinetry—Canac.

**Page 7** Series M cabinets, linear lighting, MTS sink module—Robern (photograph by Mary Nichols).

**Page 8, Top right:** *Designer: Marty Fahey, of NuHaus, 1665 Old Skokie Rd., Highland Park, IL 60035; 847-831-1330.* Model 700BR with sandblasted glass fronts surrounded by a veneered cherry pattern—Sub-Zero. **Bottom right:** 16x16-inch Goldust floor tile, 6x6-inch Goldust and Fruit Decos on wall—Daltile.

**Page 9, Top:** Laminate flooring in Bentwood Oak, countertops in Gibralter solid surfacing in Frosty White with sandwiched edge stripe of Hunter Green Mirage—Wilsonart International. **Bottom left:** Epicure 30-inch Duel Fuel Range, Model #ERSD30—Dacor. **Bottom right:** Finial faucet with blueberry scroll handles—Kohler Co.

**Page 10, Top left:** (Photograph by Nigel Marson.) **Bottom right:** Paint "Tinsel Town" 18-O-1—Dutch Boy Paint. **Page 11, top:** Paint "Hit the Jackpot" 17-O-1—Dutch Boy Paint (photograph © Laurie Black). **Bottom:** *Designers: Diane Von Furstenberg, 745 Fifth Ave., Suite 2400, New*

*York, NY 10151; 212-753-1111 and Daniel Romualdez Architects, PC, 119 W. 23rd St., Suite 710, New York, NY 10011; 212-989-8429.* Vintage bathwhirlpool in Biscuit—Kohler Co. Natural Stone-Marble in Classic Beige and Rojo Alicante, mosaic mural tile in White, Tan, Wild Rose, and Sandalwood with White porcelain field—Daltile. Paint "White" PKG.—Dutch Boy Paint.Gibraltar solid surface in White Sand—Wilsonart International.

**Page 12** Revival whirlpool in Chamois with Revival faucet—Kohler Co. Gibraltar solid surface tub surround in Light Beige—Wilsonart International.

MASTER BATH

**Pages 14-15** *Designer: Cynthia Retzlaff, Lake Mills, WI 53551.* Memoirs lavatory and toilet in Biscuit—Kohler Co. Bathroom Floor & Walls—Antique Terra Cotta from France on floor and walls, 4x4 Giallo Verona Marble Pavimenti tile on shower floor and walls, Talisman handmade tile used for border trim—Ann Sacks.

**Page 16** *Designer: Gay Fly, ASID, CKD, CBD. 6237 Cedar Creek Dr., Houston, TX 77057; 713-461-6399.* Seawall whirlpool in Biscuit, Pillow Talk lavatory in Biscuit, Neuville faucets—Kohler Co.

Classic Limestone tile—Ann Sacks.

**Page 17** *Designer: Jan Bernson.* Watersilk whirlpool in Black Black, Pillow Talk pedestal lavatory, Taboret faucets—Kohler Co. Paint "Candlewood Hill" 30-G-5—Dutch Boy Paint.

**Pages 18-19** Memoirs bath whirlpool, toilet, pedestal lavatory, and shower receptor in Biscuit; Finial faucets; Focal Neo-angle shower enclosure—Kohler Co.

**Pages 20-21** Portrait bath whirlpool, pedestal lavatory, and toilet in Teal; Antique faucets—Kohler Co. Tile—Ann Sacks. Chaise—Baker Furniture. Wall paint "Iso Taupe" 4-R-2, trim paint "Country Fairgrounds" 32-R-2—Dutch Boy Paint.

**Page 22** *Designer: Jack Weyna, ASID JKW Design Center, 218 S. Grove, Oak Park, IL 60302; 708-383-0492.* Revival mirror, Revival pedestal lav in Skylight, Taboret faucet—Kohler Co. Cintra Beige Limestone 12x12-inch floor tile (color #214)—

3x6-inch Running Leaf and 2x2-inch Georgian Border wall tile—Ann Sacks.

**Page 23** *Designers: Carol Lippert, ASID, and Lee I. Lippert, AIA, 580 Hawthorne Ave., Palo Alto, CA 94301 (415) 323-5961.* Series M cabinet with linear lighting, SOMM magnifying make-up mirror—Robern (photograph by Quadra Focus).

**Page 24** Gibralter solid surface vanity top in Platinum Tempest with carved edge—Wilsonart International.

**Page 25** Ceramic tile—Daltile. Sink, toilet—Kohler Co. Paint "Abbeyville Rose" 18-R-2—Dutch Boy Paint.

**Page 26** *Designer: Sheila Baker, Four Gracefield Rd., Hilton Head Island, SC 29928; 803-681-5963.* Russian Teacup pedestal lavatory, Profile Neo-Angle shower, Antique faucets—Kohler Co.

**Page 27** *Designer: Mary Reid, Kohler Co., Kohler, WI 53044.* Vessel Turnings in Stoneware, IV Georges faucets and accessories—Kohler Co. Tumbled marble tile,

4x4-inch Ross Verona Pavimenti tile—Ann Sacks. Mission Door Cabinets in Natural Maple—Canac. Paint "Cocoa Seeds" 4-Y-1—Dutch Boy Paints.

**Pages 28-29** Archeo copper bathtub and handshower, Kallista Caxton lav, bidet, and IV Georges faucet—Kohler Co. Wall and floor tile—Ann Sacks. Countertop—Wilsonart International.

**Page 29** Infinity bath whirlpool in white, Taboret faucet—Kohler Co. Wall paint "Sandy Oasis" 5-Y-1, trim paint "White" PKG.—Dutch Boy Paint.

**Page 30** Acrica Neo-Angle shower enclosure, Profile receptor—Kohler Co. Wall tile 4x4-inch in Chamois—Daltile.

**Page 31** Body-Spa 10-Jet System—Kohler Co. Paint—Dutch Boy.

**Pages 32-33** Pristine tub, Caxton sink, faucet—Kohler Co.

**Pages 34-35** Paint "Green Carolina" 25-B-5—Dutch Boy Paint.

**Pages 36-37** *Designer: Patricia Algiers, ASID, Kahler Slater Architects,*

*611 E. Wisconsin Ave., Milwaukee, WI 53202; 414-272-2000.* Vigora bath whirlpool and Tahoe lavatory in Jersey Cream, Cirrus faucets—Kohler Co. Tumbled marble tile—Ann Sacks. Sienna Maple cabinetry—Canac. Paint "Open Spaces" 32-Y-1—Dutch Boy Paint. Gibraltar solid surface countertop and tub surround in Natural Almond—Wilsonart International.

**Page 38** Polaris glazed 8x8-inch tile in White with undulated surfaces, 2x9-inch Blue Flores Arrow Listellos from the Meadow Series—Daltile. Paint "Chicken Scratches" 12-Y-2—Dutch Boy Paint.

**Page 39** Los Azulejos tile—Ann Sacks.

**Page 40** Wall paint "Lemon Twist KC-13, trim paint "White" PKG.—Dutch Boy Paint.

**Page 41, Top** *Designer: Lise Lawson, ASID, 6420 N. Lake Dr., Fox Point, WI 53217; 414-351-6334.* Vintage bath whirlpool in Biscuit, Antique faucet—Kohler Co.

**Bottom:** Paint "Vermont Blue" KC-23—Dutch Boy Paint. Shower wall made of SSV Solid Surfacing Veneer in Light Beige Mirage with moldings in Gibraltar Frosty White Solid Surf-acing—Wilsonart International.

**Pages 42-43** *Designer: Joanne Knaus-Sims, JKS Design Inc., 60 E. Chestnut St., Suite 375, Chicago, IL 60611; 312-642-0980.* Trocadero

vanity, shower receptor, and shower enclosure in White—Kohler Co. "Cobra Green" ungauged floor tile, Chiaro "Crater Gray" Sanded Glass wall tile—Ann Sacks. Furniture—Baker Furniture.

**Page 44** Arabesque lavatory, Tea-for-Two bath in almond—Kohler Co.

**Page 45** *Designers: Avra Bershad Pressman, ASID, and Nadine Nemec, ABID, Walnut Hill #26, Ardmore, PA 19003 (610) 642-1745.* Series M cabinet with linear incandescent lighting—Robern (photograph by Tom Crane).

THE FAMILY BATH

**Page 46** Folio Bath whirlpool, pedestal lavatory in Skylight, Finial faucets—Kohler Co. Paint "Traffic Jam" 23-V-3—Dutch Boy Paint.

**Pages 48-49** Memoirs bath, console table, and toilet in Black Black, Antique Faucet—Kohler Co. Ann Sacks Collection Tile. Wall 3x6-inch field tile, 6-inch Octagon Dot field tile—Ann Sacks.

Paint "Ultra White" PKG.—Dutch Boy Paint.Series M beveled mirror cabinet with linear incandescent lighting—Robern.

**Pages 50-51** Waterscape whirlpool in White with grip rails and pillow in Blueberry, Finial faucet—Kohler Co. Series M cabinet with Safety Lock Box—Robern (photograph by Tom Crane).

**Page 52** *Designer: Vonda Myers-Tomlinson, ASID, Kohler Co., Kohler, WI 53044.* Vessels Hex Strata lavatory in Igneous Black, Falling Water faucet—Kohler Co. Princess Limestone wall tile, Talisman Shower Square wall tile, Talisman Shadow Key wall tile, Limestone w/Metal Deco floor tile—Ann Sacks. Cellini N Monaco cabinet in Natural—Canac. Paint in Egg Shell Finish—Dutch Boy. Bath Cabinet—Robern.

THE GUEST BATH

**Page 53** Body Spa Module Bathing System with whirlpool in Innocent Blush—Kohler Co.

**Page 54** Accentials 3x3-inch wall and floor tile in Premier White and Premier Gray—Daltile. Paint "White" PKG.—Dutch Boy Paint.

**Page 55** *Designer: Jean Sedor, ASID, Jean Sedor Design, 305 South Main St., Janesville, WI 53545; 608-754-7722.* Revival Bath whirlpool, console table, and toilet in Chamois; Revival faucets—Kohler Co.

Heath Series tile in Wheat and Sea Green—Ann Sacks.

**Pages 56-57** Morningside lavatory, Finesse faucet—Kohler Co. Relief Laguna tile, 12x12-inch Chiaro Glass wall tile—Ann Sacks.

**Page 59** *Designer: Thomas Pheasant.* Revival whirlpool and lavatory in Biscuit, Revival faucets—Kohler Co. Crema Marfil floor marble—Daltile. Octagonal tray table in dark tobacco finish—McGuire Furniture.

THE POWDER ROOM

**Page 61** Peonies & Ivy lavatory, Antique faucet—Kohler Co.

**Page 62** MTS sink module—Robern (photograph by Tom Crane).

**Page 63** Series M cabinets, MPHL halogen sconce lighting, MTS sink module with all-glass lavatory—Robern (photograph by Tom Crane).

**Page 64** Caxton lavatory, Antique faucet—Kohler Co. Solid surface countertops—Wilsonart International.

**Page 66** Vessels Hex Strata lavatory in Igneous Black, Finial faucet—Kohler Co.

**Page 67** Memoirs toilet and pedestal lavatory in Jersey Cream, Revival faucet—Kohler Co. Upper wall paint "White" PKG., lower

wall paint "American Ingenuity" 15-V-3—Dutch Boy Paint.

**Page 68** Series M cabinets stacked vertically with linear incandescent lighting—Robern (photograph by Tom Crane).

**Page 70** Epernay toilet and pedestal lavatory, Antique faucets—Kohler Co. Paint Durham Beige 32-Y-5—Dutch Boy Paint.

**Page 71** Vessels Turnings lavatory in Cobalt Blue, Falling Water faucet—Kohler Co. Chiaro Glass 12x12-inch tile—Ann Sacks.

THE KIDS' BATH

**Page 72** Centerpiece lavatory in Skylight, Provence faucet—Kohler Co. Field Tile in Color #100, 4x4-inch Zoo Gang Decos. Mission Door cabinets in natural maple—

Canac. Paint "White" PKG.—Dutch Boy Paint.

**Pages 74-75 Left:** *Designers: Avra Bershad Pressman, ASID, and*

*Nadine Nemec (see page 45).* Series M beveled mirrored cabinet—Robern (photograph by Tom Crane).

**Right:** *Designer: Thomas Bartlett, Thomas Bartlett Interiors Inc, 2151 Main St., Napa, CA 94559; 707-259-1234.* Hand painting of cabinetry and mirror—Lisa Winslow, 54 Springview Ct., San Ramon, CA 94589. Drapery trim—Pierre Deus; for store locations write 870 Madison Ave., New York, NY 10021; or call 212-5709343 (photograph by Jon Jensen).

**Pages 76-77** *Designer: Cheryl Lee Janz, ASID, The Janz Group, Inc., 6173 Heritage Lane, Lisle, IL 60532; 630-369-0972.* Sonata bath/shower, Caxton lavatory, and Wellworth toilet in White; Paladar and Master Shower faucets—Kohler Co. Capriccio tile in White, Fish Seashell and Water Fantasy tile—Ann Sacks. Flashlight Yellow paint and "Lemon

Twist" KC-13—Dutch Boy Paint. Series M cabinets with linear incandescent lighting—Robern. Countertop in Designer White with

custom inset—Wilsonart.

**Page 77** Primary toilet seats—Kohler Co.

**Page 78** Precedence bath whirlpool and Cabernet wall-mount lavatory in Tender Grey, Revival faucets and accessories—Kohler Co. Tile in Ice Grey and Tender Grey—Daltile. Paint "White" PKG.—Dutch Boy Paint.

**Pages 80-81** Lakeside kitchen sink and Portofino bar sink in Almond, Antique faucets—Kohler Co. Refrigeration 700 Series—Sub-Zero. Countertop in Light Beige—Wilsonart.

THE EAT-IN KITCHEN

**Page 82** Cellini Virginian cabinetry in Sandstone—Canac.

**Pages 84-87**

*Designer: Dan McFadden, Past Basket Kitchen Designs, 765F Woodlake Rd., Kohler, WI 53044; 414-459-9976.* Hawthorne kitchen sink and Undertone bar sink, Revival faucets—Kohler Co. Backsplash 4x4-inch glazed ceramic tile in color B-01—Ann Sacks. Mission Maple cabinetry in natural finish—Canac. Oven #CPS130, cooktop #SGM3465—Dacor. Paint "White" PKG.—Dutch Boy Paint. Refrigerator Model 550—Sub-Zero. Accessories—Betty Johnson Interiors and Past Basket—765F Woodlake Rd., Kohler, WI 53044. (photograph by Susan Gilmore).

**Page 88** *Designer: Monte Berkoff, CKD,*

CR, *Herbert P. Bisulk, Inc., 295 Nassau Blvd. So., Garden City, NY 11530; 516-483-0377.* Refrigerator Model #532 with painted furniture hardwood fronts—Sub-Zero.

**Page 89** Cellini Virginian cabinetry in sandstone—Canac.

**Pages 90-91** *Designer: Marty S. Matson, Metro Design, 808 Lady St., Columbia, SC 29201; 803-252-1338.* Paint "Tinsel Town" 18-O-1—Dutch Boy Paint. Refrigerator Model #550 with front black laminate panels—Sub-Zero. Island countertop—Wilsonart (photographs by Robert Starling).

**Pages 92-93** Wall paint "Sandy Oasis" 5-Y-1, trim paint "White" PKG.—Dutch Boy Paint.

**Pages 94-95** *Designer: Michael De Guilio, De Giulio Kitchen Design, Inc., 1121 Central Ave., Wilmette, IL 60091; 847-256-8833.* Refrigerator Model #532SS—Sub-Zero (photograph by Scott McDonald, © Hedrich-Blessing).

THE COOK'S KITCHEN

**Page 96** *Designer: Missi Triplett, CKD, 990 Fifth Ave. North, Naples, FL 34102; 941-263-0403.* Range and cooktop—Dacor. Refrigerator Model #511 with stainless steel fronts—Sub-Zero. (photograph by Timm Stamm, Photography, Inc.).

**Page 97** Antique Lav faucet handles—Kohler Co. Custom Gothic Tile with fish motif—Ann Sacks.

**Page 98** Undertone prep tray sink, Coralais faucet—Kohler Co. Laminate countertops in Frosty White with custom edge in Winchester Walnut—Wilsonart.

**Page 99** Delafield kitchen sink in White, Antique faucet—Kohler Co. Paint "Marble Tile" 4-O-2—Dutch Boy Paint. Laminate countertop in Frosty White—Wilsonart.

**Page 100** *Architect : William Lipsey, River Studio Architects, 414 North Mill St., Aspen, CO 81611; 970-925-3734. Designer: Ricki Brown, CKD, Modern Kitchen Center, 5050 County Rd. 154, Glenwood Springs, CO 81601; 970-945-9194.* Cooktop Model #ESG486, Epicure Series hood, warming oven Model #EDW030—Dacor. Paint "White" PKG.—Dutch Boy Paint. Refrigerator Model #501R and #501F with stainless steel fronts—Sub-Zero.

**Page 101** Galleon kitchen sink and Aperitif bar sink in Timberline, Revival faucets—Kohler Co. Moore Merkowitz 6x6-inch Creme field tile, Moore Merkowitz 6x6-inch Creme and Green Animal tile—Ann Sacks.

**Page 102** Countertop made of SSV Solid Surfacing Veneer in Frosty White, custom edge in Hunter Green Mirage Gibraltar—Wilsonart.

**Page 103** Accentials 3x3-inch floor and wall tile in Arctic White and Cobalt Mist—Daltile.

**Page 104** Iron Tones kitchen sinks in Skylight with Provence faucet, Ravinia stainless steel sink and bar sink with Taboret faucet—Kohler Co. Laminate countertop—Wilsonart.

**Page 105** Interlace kitchen sink, Antique faucet—Kohler Co.

**Page 106.** Cilantro kitchen sink in Iron Cobalt, Coralais faucet—Kohler Co.

**Page 107** Madrigal kitchen sink in Teal, Essex faucet—Kohler Co. Wall tile in Teal and White—Daltile. Wall paint "White" PKG., trim paint "Beach Party" 20-O-1—Dutch Boy Paint. Gibraltar solid surface countertops in White Sand—Wilsonart.

**Page 108** Stainless Steel Convection Plus Single Wall oven—Dacor. Sealed Gas metal Cooktop with electric module in satin—Dacor. Wall paint "Marble Tile" 4-O-2, trim paint "White" PKG.—Dutch Boy Paint (photograph by Beth Singer).

**Page 110** Assure barrier-free kitchen sink in Desert Bloom, Colarais faucet—Kohler Co. Laminate countertop—Wilsonart.

**Page 111** Tudor Pattern Basque Slate—Ann Sacks.Ceran electric cooktop—Dacor.

**Page 112** *Designer: Ellen Cheever, CKD, CBD, Heritage Custom Kitchens, 215 Diller Ave., New Holland, PA 17557; 717-354-4011.* Entree kitchen sink in Teal, Essex faucet—Kohler Co. Floral Oswego Art Tile Mural with Custom Bisque Tile—Ann Sacks.

**Page 113** *Designer: Larry Bogdanow, AIA, L. Bogdanow & Associates, 75 Spring St.,New York, NY 10012; 212-966-0313.* Antique French Terra Cotta tile—Ann Sacks. Wall paint "White" PKG., trim paint "Sandy

Oasis" 5-Y-1—Dutch Boy Paint.

**Page 114** Vessels Iron Bell lavatory in Mexican Sand with Antique faucet—Kohler Co.

**Page 115** Mariposa bath whirlpool in Almond, Wellworth toilet in White—Kohler Co.

**Page 116** *Designers: Avra Bershad Pressman, ASID, and Nadine Nemec.* Series M cabinets with linear incandescent lighting—Robern (photograph by Tom Crane).

**Page 117** Tile Topiary Series—Ann Sacks.

**Page 118** Illustrations by Jim Swanson.

**Page 120** Aviary kitchen sink, Antique faucet—Kohler Co. Polaris 8x8-inch glazed tile in Polaris White,

Siena 4x8-inch Listellos from the Rialto Series, 1x8-inch Accent Ropes in Verde—Daltile. Paint "Cocoa Seeds" 4-Y-1—Dutch Boy Paint.

**Page 121** *Designer: Leone Nell Smets.* Refrigerator Model #550 with lacewood and white oak fronts—Sub-Zero. Pinnacle Raised Vent with Sealed Glass Gas Cooktop in Black—Dacor (photograph by Aaron Usher III).

# write away!

Now that you've had the chance to peruse the preceding pages, discover more about Kohler and their partners. When you request the literature offered on these pages, you're sure to receive more than information; inspiration will come your way as well.

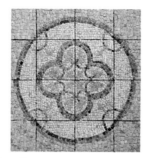

KOHLER CO.
Kohler Bath & Kitchen Ideas, a complete set of full-color product catalogs covering baths and whirlpools, showers, lavatories, toilets and bidets, kitchen and entertainment sinks, faucets, and accessories, is available for $8.00. To order, call 1-800-4-KOHLER, Ext. QV1. Internet address: www.kohlerco.com

ANN SACKS
Ann Sacks Tile and Stone has a wide selection of authentic antiquities, one-of-a-kind art tiles, mosaics, natural stone, terra cotta and signature Ann Sacks Collection tiles, manufactured exclusively in its Portland, Oregon tile studio.

A 160-page, full-color catalog will spark your creativity, and is only $18.00. Likewise, a brochure will give you an overview of some of our programs and is available for $2.00.

To order, call 503-281-7751. Internet address: www.annsacks-tile.com

CANAC
Amazing New Kitchen Ideas… Terrific tips… expert advice…and more! Canac's full-color "Kitchen Planner" is the ultimate guide for creating the kitchen you've always wanted. Easy to read and loaded with pictures, Canac's exciting new "Kitchen Planner" covers it all.

To order, please send your name and address along with a $6 check (payable to Canac Kitchens) to: Canac Kitchen Planner, 360 John St., Thornhill, ON Canada, L3T 3M9.

DACOR

Dacor, the distinctive Appliance Corporation, offers top-of-the line pure convection ovens, innovative electric and sealed-gas cooktops, duel-fuel ovens and ranges, as well as overhead and downdraft ventilation systems.

For more information, call 818-799-1000 or write to Dacor, 950 S. Raymond Ave., Pasadena, CA 91109. Internet address: www.dacorappl.com

DALTILE

An endless array of colors, a stunning display of textures. Whether you're looking for soft, subtle floral patterns, rugged, rustic natural stone looks, vibrant jewel-toned mosaics, or something in between, no one can offer you more choices than Daltile.

Call us at 1-800-933-TILE for more information, literature or product samples. Internet address: www.daltile.com

DUTCH BOY

Dutch Boy's "Kitchen and Bath Colors" brochure shows how to put together Dutch Boy paint colors in attractive, easy-to-use combinations that correspond to the colors recommended in the Kohler "Color Coordinates" program. To order, call 1-800-828-5669.

ROBERN

Find out more about fine mirrored bath cabinetry. A 24-page color booklet featuring Robern's mirrored bath cabinets, lighting, and accessories is available to you at no charge.

A complete product binder with color literature, pricing, specifications, and design ideas is available for $19.99.

To order, call 215/826-9800 or write Robern, 7 Wood Ave., Bristol, PA 19007. Internet address: www.robern.com.

SUB-ZERO

Built-in refrigeration never looked so good. Sub-Zero offers a complete line of products for your unique needs. From their classic 500 Series of built-in units, to their revolutionary 700 Series of integrated refrigeration, to their professional stainless steel models, Sub-Zero has it all.

Call or write for free catalogs. See page 122 for address and phone number.

WILSONART INTERNATIONAL

A series of idea and information brochures about Wilsonart floors, countertop surfaces, and tub and shower walls is available by simply calling the toll-free consumer hotline at 1-800-433-3222, and asking for the "Kohler Coordinates Kit." Internet address: www.wilsonart.com.

# indulgences

I'VE BEEN PERUSING BATH SHOPS LATELY. IT really comes as no surprise because I spend a lot of time in my own bath, be it literally or just in my imagination.

At the end of a long day, my mind drifts upstairs to the tub where I can all but touch a favorite book at bathside and smell the scented candles. Thick towels are waiting there, too, alongside a comfy robe and slippers.

More often than not, that sumptuous experience has to be put on hold for a while; dinner needs to be made, dogs have to be walked, and paperwork beckons from the office. Still, I get a certain amount of enjoyment just from luxuriating there in my mind.

Make no mistake—I do eventually get to that part of the day when I self-ishly indulge myself. And invariably, I find it was worth every minute's wait. Any problems of the day are immedi-ately washed away along with thoughts of everything I have to accomplish tomorrow.

It's such a simple ritual but an important one, too. In fact, just thinking about it, I....

Excuse me, I suddenly have to be somewhere else.

Heather J. Paper
Project Editor